How We Live Is How We Die

Books by Pema Chödrön

Awakening Loving-Kindness
Becoming Bodhisattvas
Comfortable with Uncertainty
The Compassion Book
Living Beautifully
The Places That Scare You
The Pocket Pema Chödrön
Practicing Peace
Start Where You Are
Taking the Leap
Welcoming the Unwelcome
When Things Fall Apart
The Wisdom of No Escape

How We
Live Is How
We Die

Pema Chödrön

EDITED BY

Joseph Waxman

SHAMBHALA

Shambhala Publications, Inc.
2129 13th Street
Boulder, Colorado 80302
www.shambhala.com

Cover photo: "Forest Golden Hour" by A.J. Schokora/Stocksy
Cover design: Daniel Urban-Brown
Interior design: Lora Zorian

9 8 7 6 5 4 3 2

Printed in the United States of America

Shambhala Publications makes every effort to print on
acid-free, recycled paper.
Shambhala Publications is distributed worldwide by
Penguin Random House, Inc., and its subsidiaries.

Copyright page continued on page 222

This book is dedicated
with love and great appreciation
to my dear sister, Patricia Billings,
who died at age ninety-one in February 2020.

Contemplating death five times a day brings happiness.

—BHUTANESE SAYING

Contents

Introduction

The Buddha famously advised his students not to buy in to everything he said without first checking it out for themselves. He wanted to promote firsthand experience, not dogma. "Don't just take my word for it," he said. "Examine my teachings the way a goldsmith examines gold." For instance, the Buddha taught that focusing too much on our own self-interest brings us pain and anxiety, and that extending our love and care toward others—even strangers or those who cause us trouble—brings us joy and peace. This is something we can verify through our own experience. We can experiment with this teaching; we can test it as many times as is necessary for us to be convinced.

The teachings presented in this book, however, appear to be in another category. The Tibetan word *bardo*, which will frequently come up, commonly refers to the passage following our death and preceding our next life. But how can we verify from our own experience what happens after we die? How can we verify that there will be a next life? In these chapters, you will find descriptions of brightly colored lights, of deafening sounds, of hungry ghosts, of peaceful and wrathful deities. How is it possible to examine such teachings the way a goldsmith examines gold?

My intention is not to convince you to buy in to the Tibetan worldview and to see such descriptions as the definitive truth about what happens after you die. To say anything is definitively "like this" or "like that" somehow misses the point. I feel it goes against the spirit of the Buddha's teachings. At the same time, many discerning people alive today study the bardo teachings and take them seriously—not as an academic subject but as a source of profound wisdom that enhances their lives. It may not be possible for us to confirm these traditional teachings based on our firsthand experience. But whether or not we believe in the Tibetan worldview, if we get to the essence of the bardo teachings, they can benefit us not only after we die, but this year, this day, this moment.

These teachings are based on an ancient Tibetan text called *Bardo Tödrol*, which was first translated into English as *The Tibetan Book of the Dead* but which literally means "liberation through hearing in the intermediate [or in-between] state." *Bardo Tödrol* is meant to be read to those who have passed away and entered this state. It describes the various experiences the dead person will go through and thus serves as a guide to help them navigate what is thought to be a disorienting journey from this life to the next life. The idea is that hearing the *Bardo Tödrol* will optimize one's chances for a peaceful death, a peaceful journey, and a favorable rebirth. In the best-case scenario, one will be liberated altogether from samsara, the painful cycle of birth and death.

The term *bardo* is usually associated with the intermediate state between lives, but a broader translation of the word is simply "transition" or "gap." The journey that takes place after our death is one such transition, but when we examine our experience closely, we will find that we are always in transition. During every moment of our lives, something is ending and something else is beginning. This is not an esoteric concept. When we pay attention, it becomes our unmistakable experience.

The Tibetan Book of the Dead lists six bardos: the natural bardo of this life, the bardo of dreaming, the bardo of meditation, the bardo of dying, the bardo of *dharmata*, and the bardo of becoming.

Right now we are in the natural bardo of this life. As I will continue to emphasize throughout this book, the natural bardo of this life is where our work lies. By coming to understand how this life is a bardo—a state of continual change—we will be ready to face any other bardos that may arise, however unfamiliar.

The bardo of dying begins when we realize we're going to die and lasts until our final breath. This is followed by the bardo of dharmata, which means "the true nature of phenomena." Finally, there is the bardo of becoming, during which we make the transition to our next life. In this book, I will talk about these three bardos in detail and also connect them to more familiar experiences that we go through during our lives.

My aspiration for what follows is to write in such a way that you will find these teachings meaningful and helpful, whatever your beliefs. At the same time, I'd like to encourage you to "lean your openness" toward the less familiar aspects of these teachings, as my teacher Dzigar Kongtrul Rinpoche likes to say. I've always found that my greatest personal growth happens when my mind and heart are more curious than doubtful; my hope is that you will take a similar approach to reading this book.

If we can learn to navigate the continual flow of transitions in our present life, we will be prepared for our death and whatever may follow, no matter what worldview we subscribe to. My teachers, beginning with Chögyam Trungpa Rinpoche, have given me many instructions in how to do this. I have learned from experience that applying these bardo teachings has removed much of my fear and anxiety about death. But just as importantly, this training has made me feel more alive, open, and courageous in my day-to-day experience of life. This is why I would like to pass these teachings and their benefits on to you.

How We Live Is How We Die

1

———

The Wondrous Flow
of Birth and Death

This is a book about fear of death. More accurately, this book presents a question: How do we relate to the most fundamental of all fears, the fear of death? Some people banish the thought of death from their minds and act as if they will live forever. Some tell themselves that life is the only thing that matters since death—in their view—equals nothingness. Some become obsessed with their health and safety and base their lives on staving off the unavoidable for as many years as possible. It is less common for people to open themselves fully to the inevitability of their death—and any fear that may provoke—and to live their lives accordingly.

I have found that those who do open themselves in this way are more engaged in life and more appreciative of what they have. They are less caught up in their own dramas and have a more beneficial effect on other people and on the planet as a whole. These people include my teachers as well as the sages from all the world's spiritual traditions. But there are many ordinary people who neither deny nor obsess over death, however; instead, they live in harmony with the certain knowledge that they will one day depart from this world.

A few years ago, I gave a weekend seminar on this topic at the Omega Institute in Rhinebeck, New York. One of the participants admitted to me that when she first heard I was going to talk about death and dying, her reaction was "Bummer!" By the end of the program, however, she was finding the subject matter to be life-changing. My hope, in sharing these teachings, is to help you become more familiar and at ease with death, and more able to live in harmony with what previously scared you—more able to move from "Bummer!" to breakthrough.

My second, closely related aspiration is that opening to death will help you open to life. As I will repeat in the pages that follow, death is not just something that happens at the end of our life. Death happens every moment. We live in a wondrous flow of birth and death, birth and death. The end of one experience is the beginning of the next experience, which quickly comes to its own end, leading to a new beginning. It's like a river continuously flowing.

Usually, we resist this flow by trying to solidify our experience in one way or another. We try to find something, anything, to hold on to. The instruction here is to relax and let go. The training here is to accustom ourselves to existing within this continuous flow. This is the way to work with our fears about death and about life and allow them to melt away. This isn't a guarantee; you can't ask for your money back if it doesn't happen, or if it takes longer than you would like. But I have been moving slowly in this direction and I think you can as well.

In the Mahayana tradition of Buddhism that I follow, it's customary to begin any study, practice, or other positive activity by contemplating its greater purpose. We could reflect, for instance, on the benefit that making friends with the flow of birth and death might bring to our immediate surroundings, to the people in our lives—and even beyond. We could reflect on how our deepening relaxation with life and death could positively impact all that we encounter.

As an illustration of how interconnected our world is, the chaos theorists say that a butterfly flapping its wings in the Amazon affects the weather in Europe. Just like that, our state of mind affects the world. We know how it affects the people around us. If you scowl at someone, they're more likely to scowl at another person. If you smile at them, it makes them feel good and they're more likely to smile at others. Similarly, if you become more at ease with the transitory quality of life and the inevitability of death, that ease will be transmitted to others.

Any positive energy we put toward ourselves or others creates an atmosphere of love and compassion that ripples out and out—who knows how far? With this in mind, we could come to this exploration of death with our best self, the self that is sensitive to the fears and pains of our fellow beings and wants to help. To support this aspiration, we could dedicate this particular journey through the bardo for the well-being of at least one other person who's having difficulties. You could start by writing down a few names and add more as time goes on. In the end, you may find yourself with a list that is many pages long.

Billions of people on this planet need care and support. We can wish that whatever progress we make will somehow give them a bit of the help they need. We may only be able to help a small number of people directly, but everyone can be included in our aspirations.

Establishing our motivation in this way is known as "generating *bodhichitta*," the heart of compassion, or as Dzigar Kongtrul Rinpoche calls it, "the mindset of awakening." We educate ourselves in the Dharma not only to help ourselves, but to help the world.

2

Continual Change

Some people believe that consciousness ends at the moment of death. Others believe it continues. What everyone can agree on, however, is that during our present lifetime, things definitely keep going. And as they keep going, they continually change. Things are constantly coming to an end, and things are constantly coming into being. There is a continual process of death and renewal, death and renewal. This experience, which every living being goes through, is what is known as "impermanence."

The Buddha stressed impermanence as one of the most important contemplations on the spiritual path. "Of all footprints, the elephant's are outstanding," he said. "Just so, of all subjects of meditation . . . the idea of impermanence is unsurpassed."

Contemplating impermanence is the perfect way into the bardo teachings, and the teachings on death altogether. This is because, compared to those more difficult topics, continual change is easy to see and understand. The seasons change, the days change, the hours of the day change. We ourselves change all along, and we experience many changes from moment to moment. This happens all around us and within us, twenty-four seven, never stopping for an instant.

Still, for some reason, we don't fully appreciate what's going on. We tend to behave as if things are more fixed than they really are. We're under the illusion that life will stay similar to how it is now. A vivid recent example has been the coronavirus pandemic. We took for granted that the world would keep going in a certain way, and then everything was suddenly turned on its head in ways we couldn't even imagine.

Despite our lifetime of experience with change, something within us never stops insisting on stability. Any change, even a change for the better, can feel a little unnerving because it seems to expose our underlying uncertainty about life. We'd rather think we have firm ground to stand on than see clearly that everything is always in transition. We'd rather deny the reality of continual change than accept the way things are.

Holding on to the feeling of permanence also happens with our emotional states. Whether we feel good or bad, happy or sad, optimistic or pessimistic, we tend to forget that feelings are fleeting. It's as if there's a mechanism that blocks us from remembering everything is always in flux. Our current state of anxiety or elation just seems to be how our life is. When we're happy, we become disappointed when our good feeling fades away; when we're unhappy, we feel stuck in our unpleasant emotions. So whether we feel good or bad, our illusion of permanence leads to problems.

The Buddha spoke about our difficulty accepting impermanence when he taught on the three types of suffering. He called the first type "the suffering of suffering." This is the blatant agony of war, starvation, terrifying environments, abuse, neglect, tragic loss, or a series of severe illnesses. It's what we usually think of when we talk about "pain" or "suffering." The people and animals who are in these situations go from one suffering to the next with hardly a break.

Some people are fortunate enough not to be experiencing the blatant suffering of suffering. Compared to what others are going through, currently things are pretty good. But we still have the pain that comes from the fact that nothing lasts. We experience delight, but it alternates with disappointment. We experience fulfillment, but it alternates with boredom. We experience pleasure, but it alternates with discomfort. This alternation, and all the hope and fear it brings up, is itself a great source of pain.

This second type of suffering, which the Buddha simply called "the suffering of change," lurks in our gut as the painful knowledge that we can never really get all that we want. We can never get our life to be just the way we want it to be, once and for all. We can never reach a position where we're always feeling good. We may sometimes feel comfortable and satisfied, but as my daughter once remarked, "That's the problem." Because things go well for us just often enough, we keep coming back to the false hope that we could keep it going that way. We think, "If I just do everything right, I can always feel great!" I think this is some of what's behind drug abuse and all our other addictions. The underlying addiction is to this dream of lasting pleasure and comfort.

All the world's religions and wisdom traditions speak about the futility of striving for happiness by investing ourselves in things that don't last. When we hear these teachings, they don't surprise us and for a while we may even feel convinced by them. We may even start to think it's ridiculous to strive for happiness in such a fruitless way. But as soon as we think of a new thing we want, all this wisdom tends to go out the window. And then it's just a matter of time before impermanence spoils our brand-new thing. Even if we don't spill coffee on it the morning after it arrives, our pleasure fades away some time in the not-too-distant future.

The classic example is falling in love. In the beginning, it's the greatest high there could ever be. From there, it can easily turn into the greatest disappointment. When the high fades away, if the lovers want to stay together, they need to overcome their disappointment and go deeper with their relationship. Many couples manage this transition beautifully, but even so, that initial absolute pleasure of two people falling in love is over.

The third type of suffering, known as "all-pervasive suffering," happens at a deeper and subtler level than the first two. This is the constant discomfort that comes from our basic resistance to life as it really is. We want some solid ground to rely on, but that's just not in the cards. The reality is that nothing ever stays still, even for an instant. When we examine very closely, we see that even the most apparently stable things are constantly changing. Everything is on the move, and we never know which direction things are headed. If even mountains and boulders are unpredictably moving and changing, how can we find security in anything? This constant feeling of groundlessness and insecurity quietly pervades every moment of our life. It is the subtle discomfort that underlies both the suffering of suffering and the suffering of change.

Again, we can look at falling in love. A big part of the thrill is the freshness this new love brings to our life.

Our entire world feels fresh. But as time goes on, we start wanting everything to remain exactly the way we like it to be. This is when all-pervasive suffering rears its head and the honeymoon phase comes to an end. As the freshness fades away, the lovers begin to notice certain things, such as how the other one is stingy or overcritical. Somehow the veil is lifted and they begin to find each other irritating, just for being how they are. What often happens next is they start trying to improve each other, to make their partner shape up. But that approach only makes things worse. The only way relationships really work is when both people are able to let things be and work with each other as they are. This means overcoming some of their general resistance to life as it is—rather than life as they want it to be.

We often hear people say things like "Don't worry, it will all work out." I've always taken this to be an attempt to reassure us that things will eventually work out the way *we* want them to. But, so much of the time, we don't get what we want, and even when we do, our pleasure is only fleeting. And much of the time, we get what we *don't* want— ah, the vicissitudes of life.

Trungpa Rinpoche had a saying about this: "Trust not in success. Trust in reality." Believing things will work out the way we want them to is "trusting in success"—success on our terms. But from our own experience, we know very well that success is unreliable. Sometimes things do work out in the manner we like; sometimes they don't. "Trusting in reality" is a much more open and relaxed frame of mind. Reality is going to take place, one way or another. We can count on it. It is actually very profound and, at the same time, completely straightforward. "Reality" refers to things just as they are, free of our hopes and fears. Knowing this to be the case, we can be open to pleasure and pain, success and failure—as opposed to feeling subjected to a personal vendetta when we don't get the job, when we don't get the partner, when we get sick. This is a radical approach; it goes completely against our conventional way of looking at things. We can be open to both the wanted and the unwanted. We know that they will change, just as the weather will change. And, like good and bad weather, success and failure are equally part of life.

All-pervasive suffering is our constant struggle against the fact that everything is wide-open, that we never know what's going to happen, that our life is unwritten and unfolds as we go along, and that there's very little we can do to control it. We experience this struggle as a persistent hum of anxiety in the background of our life. This all comes from the fact that everything is impermanent. Everything in the universe is in flux. The solid ground we walk on changes from instant to instant.

However, as Thich Nhat Hanh says, "It's not impermanence that makes us suffer. What makes us suffer is wanting things to be permanent when they are not." We can continue to resist reality, or we can learn to frame things in a new way, seeing our life as dynamic and vibrant, an amazing adventure. Then we will truly be in contact with the freshness of each moment, whether we think our lover is perfect or not. If we can embrace continual change in this way, we'll start to notice the hum of anxiety quieting down and slowly, slowly fading away.

3

Passing Memory

During some of the retreats I lead, we recite this chant in the morning: "Like a shooting star, a visual fault, a candle flame, an illusion, a dewdrop, a water bubble, a dream, lightning, a cloud: regard conditioned dharmas like that." This verse is meant to impress impermanence on our minds so we can get used to its presence in our lives—and so we can learn to become friends with it. "Conditioned dharmas" means anything that has come into being: anything that has begun and is in the process of changing and at a certain point will end—in other words, all phenomena. Everything under the sun has the fleeting quality of a dewdrop or a flash of lightning. At the retreats, I recommend that people memorize this chant so they can say it to themselves and contemplate it as they walk around the land and when they return home.

Realizing the fleeting nature of everything and the freshness of every moment is equivalent to realizing that we're always in a state of transition, an in-between state—what we call a "bardo." A few years ago, I was having lunch with Anam Thubten Rinpoche, a Tibetan teacher I admire greatly. I brought with me a whole list of questions about the bardo and what *The Tibetan Book of the Dead* says about it. I was asking him my questions and at one point, he said to me, "You know, Ani Pema, we're always in the bardo." I had heard this notion expressed by Trungpa Rinpoche, but I wanted to hear Anam Thubten's explanation, so I said, "Well, Rinpoche, you and I are sitting here having lunch. How is this the bardo?"

I've written about this elsewhere, but his response made such an impression on me that I think it bears repeating. "This morning," he said, "I went to the art store with my friend to buy materials for doing calligraphy. We bought some ink and brushes and paper. Now that experience seems like a past lifetime, a whole lifetime of its own. It had a beginning, which was like being born. Then it lasted for a while and went through different phases: looking around the store, picking out the supplies, paying for them. Then my friend and I parted and that lifetime came to an end. Now it's all just a memory and here I am eating lunch with you, enjoying another lifetime. Soon this lifetime will come to an end and turn into another memory. And this process of beginnings and endings, births and deaths, will never cease. It will go on and on and on, forever."

We are always in a bardo because impermanence never takes a break. There is never a moment when we're not in transition—and believe it or not this is good news. The elements that make up this unique moment of your life all came into being at some point; soon those elements will disperse and this experience will be over. Right now you may be sitting in your chair reading this book or driving in your car and listening to the audio version. Wherever you are, the light has its own particular quality. You are smelling particular smells and hearing particular sounds in the background. An hour ago, you were probably doing something completely different, something you can only partially remember. An hour from now, this current experience will also be a memory. We're always in an intermediate state between the past and the future, between the memory of what happened before and the approaching experience that will soon become memory as well.

My lunch that day with Anam Thubten will never happen again. Even if I have another lunch with him in the same place and we have the same meal and talk about the same subjects, we will never be able to re-create what happened last time. That hour is gone forever.

Contemplating continual change is a poignant experience. It can feel sad or scary. Sometimes, when I'm in a long retreat and every day I do pretty much the same thing, I suddenly realize, "It's Sunday again? How could that possibly be? It just was Sunday!" I want time to slow down. The speed at which it moves just takes my breath away. This feeling is especially strong in my old age. When I think back to my childhood, the summer was so long. Now it's over in the blink of an eye. It's good to let that feeling sink in. That vulnerable, tender feeling needs to be felt and allowed in.

Feeling sad or anxious is natural when we reflect on the passage of time and the fading of all our experiences. In the evocative words of Trungpa Rinpoche, all our experiences are "passing memory." It can be heartbreaking to notice how death and loss are occurring continually. It can make us feel shaky to realize we are always in a gap. But these feelings aren't a sign of something being wrong. We don't have to push them away. We don't have to label them as negative or reject them in any way. Instead, we can develop open-heartedness to our painful emotions around impermanence. We can learn to sit with these feelings, to become curious about them, to see what vulnerability has to offer. In that very fear, in that very melancholy, is our compassionate heart, our immeasurable wisdom, our connection to all other living beings on this planet, each of whom are going through their own bardos. When we stay present with our transitory experience and all that its fleetingness evokes, we get in touch with our braver self, our deepest nature.

One of the students at the Gampo Abbey bardo retreat had a profound and courageous way of working with this kind of sadness and discomfort. "Being in the gap is uncomfortable," she said. "It feels like it's not where you want to be. But I think it's precisely where you do want to be. You want to find a way to rest with that, and it requires a lot of bravery, intention, and commitment."

What she said captures for me the spirit of training in embracing impermanence. Instead of seeing our sadness as a problem, we can look at it as a sign that we're on to something. We're beginning to get the mood or quality of why we don't like to hang out in groundlessness. We're directly tasting our resistance to the continual flow of life.

If we keep accustoming ourselves to being present with this flow, we will gradually develop confidence that we're big enough to hold the sadness. We will gradually learn to trust reality rather than hope for "success." This is a matter of training, of building up a muscle day by day. Practicing this new approach to our existence will enable us to meet whatever happens—wanted or unwanted, health or sickness, life or death—with cheerfulness and grace.

4

How We Live Is How We Die

My friend Judith was in her thirties and married with two young children, and it was heartbreaking when she developed terminal cancer. At first, she went through the classic early stages of coming to terms with her death: denial, anger, and so on. Then the family decided to move to a small town in Colorado, near where Judith had grown up. They rented a house and the whole family and a good friend took time out just to be with Judith and support her. The children kept going to school, but outside of that, their main focus was their mother. They all talked freely about death. Fortunately, Judith had time to get used to the fact that she was going to die. She read about and contemplated the bardo teachings and became familiar with the stages of dying and with the idea that death happens at every moment. As time went on, she became happier and happier. "It doesn't make any sense," she said. "My little children are playing here, and I'm just blissfully happy."

As she became more ill, her lungs started filling with fluid and she had to sleep in a recliner. One morning, she was lying in the recliner, totally relaxed, with her husband and her friend by her side. All of a sudden, she pointed to her mouth. They asked her if she wanted some water, but she shook her head. After a few more guesses, her husband said, "Are you telling me you can't speak?" She nodded. Then she pointed to her eyes. Again, it took a few guesses for them to realize she couldn't see. Her husband immediately called the doctor. But she just lay there, happy and smiling, as calm as could be. She knew she was dying, and off she went. She was able to let impermanence unfold without resisting. Before she got sick, no one could have imagined she'd go out so smoothly—this fiery, red-headed young woman with her sharp tongue. But in the end, she came through beautifully. I would like to die like that.

If you've been in the presence of more than one person at the time of death, you will know how different the end can be for different people. I've witnessed people happily let go, with no sense of struggle, as Judith did. They are able just to go with it. I've also been with someone who resisted to the very last minute, practically screaming all along. That was a frightening experience for me. Seeing that made me think, "If there's anything I can do now to prepare, I want to do it."

I can't say for certain what happens after death, but I'm completely sure that I don't want to die as if someone's pushing me into a black pit. For that reason, I've made a strong effort over the years to practice toward my inevitable death. The idea of rebirth makes sense to me and when people ask me if I believe in it, I say that I do. But I like to add, "If it turns out not to be true, I'm ready."

Then again, we may think we're ready, but we never know until the time comes. A few years ago, I went through a virtual reality test to see how I would do in various frightening situations. I did well with flying. I did fine with reptiles and spiders. But there was one simulation where you go up about forty stories in an elevator and the doors open and you step out onto a plank. You're supposed to walk along the plank for a bit and then jump off. Outside the simulation, I was in a small room in a university standing on a board resting firmly on the floor. But my palms were sweating so profusely that I could barely hold the controls I was supposed to be operating. I inched along as if I were really forty stories up and when it got to the point where I was supposed to jump, I became paralyzed. After an embarrassingly long time, I was able to make the jump, which in reality was from half an inch off the floor.

Now I'd like to go back and walk that plank again, not because it was such a fun experience the first time but because it could help prepare me for death. Next time I would say to myself, "You're less than an inch off the floor. When you step off, nothing's going to happen, even though you appear to be forty stories up and there are all those tiny cars way below. This is a useful reality check. The groundlessness you feel now is similar to what you'll feel when you die. You might as well get used to it now."

We don't enjoy uncertainty, insecurity, and groundlessness. We don't seek out vulnerability and rawness. These feelings make us uncomfortable and we do whatever we can to avoid them. But these states of mind are always with us, if not blatantly then at least subtly, in the background. To some degree, we always sense that we're on a plank forty stories up. This is the all-pervasive suffering the Buddha described.

At various points of our lives, we experience groundlessness acutely. We move to a new place, or our children leave the house, or we receive sudden bad news. Or a flood or hurricane or fire sweeps away our whole life in a few hours. Or perhaps we have to flee our homeland, as the Tibetans did, and as countless people are doing now. We become a refugee, taking nothing with us but what we can carry, and maybe not even that. Sometimes this is totally unexpected. Out of nowhere, we lose our home, our country, our customs and traditions. And what then? Life continues, and we find ourselves in a new place, a very vulnerable place.

My most intense experience of groundlessness was quite minor compared to what is happening to so many these days. Nevertheless, it totally pulled the rug out from life as I knew it. It was many decades ago when my husband suddenly announced he was leaving me. One moment I was in a long-term marriage, the next moment I wasn't. For some time, I completely lost my bearings and didn't know who I was. I've told this story many times because in a way it was the turning point in my life that set me off toward a spiritual path. As much as I wanted things to go back to the way they used to be, I had an intuition that I'd been given a great gift.

As awful as I felt, I kept thinking to myself that this was actually the chance of a lifetime. Something just disappeared on me, leaving me in a fertile, tremendously meaningful place where anything could happen and I could go in any direction I wanted. It was almost like being twenty years old again, where you feel like you have all the world's possibilities in front of you. Of course, I vacillated for a while between this feeling of limitless possibility and the overwhelming wish to return to the familiar. But in this case, there was no way things could ever go back. My only option was to go forward, with as much bravery as I could muster, into the unknown.

Abrupt and shocking transitions can upend our world, but no experience of groundlessness is as powerful and unsettling as the end of our own life. If we aim to meet our death as calmly as Judith did, then we can try to see the other upheavals in our life as "the chance of a lifetime." Major dislocations and reversals expose the truth underlying all our experience—that there is nothing reliable to hold on to, and that our sense of a solid, stable reality is just an illusion. Every time our bubble is burst, we have a chance to become more used to the nature of how things are. If we can see these as opportunities, we'll be in a good position to face the end of our life and to be open to whatever may happen next.

How we live is how we die. For me, this is the most fundamental message of the bardo teachings. How we deal with smaller changes now is a sign of how we'll deal with bigger changes later. How we relate to things falling apart right now foreshadows how we'll relate to things falling apart when we die.

But we don't have to wait for enormous transitions to force us into reckoning with groundlessness. We can begin right away to notice the transitory nature of each day and each hour, reflecting on Anam Thubten's words about how we continually go through endings and beginnings, endings and beginnings, one mini-lifetime after another.

At the same time, we can work with our general fear and anxiety about the fact that we're not in control. Most of the time, we'd rather dwell in the illusion of control and certainty than recognize how life and death are always unpredictable. Actually, I've often asked myself, "Is it really a problem that we have so little control? Is it a problem that when we plan our day, it rarely turns out as we predicted?

Is it a problem that plans altogether are written in water?" I had my whole year scheduled when Covid hit, and as happened to millions of others, all my plans were suddenly erased like words from a blackboard.

Over the years, people say little things to you that make a big impact. Once someone said to me, almost in passing: "Life has its own natural choreography." I thought about that for a long time and started tapping into this natural choreography and experimenting with letting it do its thing. I found that most of the time, when I just leave it alone, what that choreography comes up with is much more inspired, creative, and interesting than anything my mind could come up with.

Trusting the natural choreography of life is another way of talking about trusting in reality. We can start to develop this trust by allowing ourselves to let go in small ways. For instance, when I teach, I like to experiment with allowing things just to unfold. Before I gave the talks that have gone into this book, I spent a good deal of time reading and thinking about the bardos and I jotted down various notes. But when I arrived at the retreat and the time came for me to speak in front of people, I left the notes behind and was curious if the words would even come out of my mouth. I've found that my teachings flow better if I just step into open space and leap.

If we experiment, to the best of our current ability, in letting things naturally unfold, I think we'll be pleasantly surprised. We go ahead and make our plans, but we're open to seeing them change. As a result, our insistence on predictability may steadily weaken. Sometimes our old habit will still be too seductive and it will be nearly impossible to trust the natural choreography. In those cases, the best advice I've been given is just to notice the tendency to control and to own it with kindness. This is very different from mindlessly wanting to pin everything down, with no awareness of what we're doing and no sense of its absurdity. It's just a matter of seeing our habit and not criticizing ourselves for it. This kind of simple self-reflection will also give us empathy for all the other people who want so badly to be in control—meaning just about everyone on this planet.

Habituating ourselves a little every day to the basic groundlessness of life will pay large dividends at the end of life. Somehow, despite its ongoing presence in our lives, we're still not used to continual change. The uncertainty that accompanies every day and every moment of our lives is still an unfamiliar presence. As we contemplate these teachings and pay attention to the constant, unpredictable flow of our experience, we just might start to feel more relaxed with how things are. If we can bring this relaxation to our deathbed, we will be ready for whatever may happen next.

5

When the Appearances of This Life Dissolve: The Bardo of Dying

When the appearances of this life dissolve,
May I, with ease and great happiness,
Let go of all attachments to this life
As a son or daughter returning home.

I've always found these lines by Dzigar Kongtrul Rinpoche to be very powerful, especially the image of the child returning home in a state of ease and great happiness. They refer to the process of dying, the period between when we know we are going and our last breath. I've taught this prayer to many people at the end of their lives, including a nun at Gampo Abbey who said it over and over again as she was dying. I may well do the same.

What does it mean for the appearances of this life to dissolve, and how can that become an experience of joy and peace? In the Tibetan worldview, our bodies are made of five elements: earth, water, fire, air, and space. The earth element is everything solid in the body: bones, muscles, teeth, and so on. The water element is the various fluids, such as blood, lymph, and saliva. The fire element is our body's warmth. The air element is our breath. The space element is the cavities within our body, all the open spaces. There is also a sixth, nonphysical element that comes into play: consciousness.

According to *The Tibetan Book of the Dead*, during the dying process, these elements dissolve into one another, from the grossest to the subtlest. This presentation may seem foreign or antiquated to us, but hospice workers have told me they also recognize these stages in their patients. I'll describe the traditional progression while acknowledging that both end-of-life caregivers and Tibetan teachers report that, like other life stages, the order of dissolution varies among individuals. This, too, is unpredictable.*

First, the earth element dissolves into the water element. The dying person feels heavy. Sometimes they say, "I feel like I'm sinking. Can you lift me up?" At the same time, their eyesight starts to get weaker. Next, the water element dissolves into the fire element. The liquids start drying up. The dying person feels very thirsty and will often ask for something to drink. We can't retain our fluids. Our hearing also starts to go. Then the fire element dissolves into the air element and we feel cold. No matter how high the heat is turned up, no matter how many blankets we have on, we just can't get warm. The next stage is when the air element dissolves into consciousness. It gets harder and harder to breathe. Our out-breaths get longer

---

* A chart outlining the stages of dissolution and their qualities is available in appendix C on page 188.

and our in-breaths get shorter. There are big gaps between breaths. Finally, after a few long out-breaths, our breathing comes to an end. As Trungpa Rinpoche said, "You breathe out and keep going. No more in-breath."

At this point, all ordinary sense perceptions have ceased. All thoughts, emotions, habitual patterns, and neuroses have ceased as well. Everything that had obscured our true nature is gone. Everything we considered "me" is gone. The appearances of this life have dissolved, and we have returned to the natural simplicity of our true nature.

According to Western medicine, the person is dead. Life is over. But in the Buddhist teachings, it is said that an internal process, known as the "inner dissolution," continues. In this final dissolution of our lifetime, the element of consciousness dissolves into space. This process is also unpredictable, but in general, it is said to last about twenty minutes. For this reason, the teachings recommend letting the body be, without touching or moving it, for at least that amount of time, and preferably much longer.

The inner dissolution presents us with an incredible chance, if we are prepared for it. It is said to happen in three stages during which we have three strong experiences of color. First, the light of the whole environment becomes white, like a cloudless sky lit up by a full moon. Then we perceive redness, like the sky at sunset. Finally, we perceive black, like a night sky with no moon or stars. At this point, we fall into a blank state of unconsciousness and the dissolution process is complete.

The next thing that happens, according to the teachings, is that an egoless me recovers consciousness and the mind is experienced in a completely naked, unobstructed way. This is sometimes referred to as "the mind of clear light of death." It only lasts for a moment, but as we will see, preparing for this experience can short-circuit the entire cycle of birth and death and cause full awakening on the spot. This is considered such a precious opportunity that all of my principal teachers have emphasized preparing for it as one of the most important endeavors of life.

To see how such a thing is possible requires some understanding of the innermost essence of our mind. When we talk about the awakened mind, we often use adjectives such as "wide-open," "unobstructed," "unbiased," and "infinite." But the amazing thing is these words also apply to *your* mind—as well as to your cousin's mind, your boss's mind, your irritating neighbor's mind, everybody's mind.

Traditionally, this universal awakened mind is compared to the sky. From our perspective on the ground, the sky appears clearly on some days but is obscured on others. But no matter how clouded over and dark it is, if we go up in an airplane, we see that the vast blue sky is, and always has been, right there—all day, every day.

For many of us, when it comes to this sky-like mind, the weather seems predominantly cloudy. Instead of being awake to the vibrancy of the phenomenal world and its continuous flow of birth and death, we live in a version of reality where we often feel completely distracted and lost in thought. We're not in tune with the fact that everything—from our environment to our loved ones to our very bodies—changes instant by instant. We don't see how our emotions and storylines have no real substance to them, how they are as ephemeral as mist.

These thoughts and emotions feel so solid to us that they can completely obscure the open clarity of our mind.

Once in a while, however, we may glimpse the blue sky through a gap in the clouds. This often happens when something unexpected interrupts the habitual workings of our mind. For instance, back in the eighties, I was walking down a Boulder, Colorado, street in my maroon robes, completely lost in thought. A car full of college boys drove up alongside me and one of them rolled down the window and yelled, "Get a job!" (It was especially disorienting because I happened to be walking to work.) For a moment, my habitual mind just stopped and I experienced everything in an utterly fresh way. Thanks to those boys, I experienced a major gap in the clouds.

Glimpses of the sky can come to us in many ways, but they often involve an experience of groundlessness. The sound of an explosion startles and disorients us. We almost slip on the ice. We receive some unexpected news— very bad or very good. From out of nowhere, our mind stops and we look out and there's a vivid, timeless world.

We usually have no way to make use of these brief flashes of insight. But if we have even a glimpse of the big sky, we can learn to value these experiences and start to cultivate them. You could say this is one of the main purposes of meditation: to slow down enough to notice there are always gaps in our dense, thought-filled experience— and to become familiar with these gaps as glimpses of the unfabricated, nonconceptual nature of mind.

In this way, we slowly come to realize that our mind is always wide-open and infinite. But even when we're unaware of it, it never went anywhere, and we can reconnect with it at any time. With the help of meditation practice, we begin to really understand that clouds are impermanent and that the sky is always there. As Trungpa

Rinpoche once said, "At first it takes almost being hit by a truck to wake us up, but after a while, all it takes is the wind blowing the curtain."

According to the bardo teachings, the process of dissolution during dying can be seen as a process of clouds thinning out and parting. As each stage occurs, from the dissolving of the earth element on, the clouds disperse more and more. Everything falls apart: our body, our sense perceptions, our emotions, our thinking process. This can of course feel destabilizing and frightening. But if we've practiced to become familiar with the continuous dissolving that takes place during our life, the continuous round of deaths and rebirths, then we may be able enter the dying experience fearlessly, ready to face whatever may come. When groundlessness has become familiar territory for us, the ultimate groundlessness of death will no longer feel so threatening.

We may then experience the end of this life as a falling apart into wakefulness. Through the stages of dissolution, all the clouds have vanished, revealing the pristine sky of mind in all its clarity. Right here we have an important chance, the chance to recognize this vast sky-like awareness as our own innate nature and then let go and relax into that state, like a child returning home.

For most people, however, this opportunity comes and goes in a flash. Everyone without exception—even the smallest insect—has a fleeting experience of infinitely open awareness, but it is said that very few recognize it. So it passes by unnoticed. One of the main reasons *The Tibetan Book of the Dead* and other bardo teachings exist is to prepare people to recognize what is going on during the death process so they can recognize the opportunities when they arise. As we'll see in later chapters, the time of dissolution is not our only chance to attain enlightenment during the death process. Luckily for us, even in the bardo, it's never too late to try again.

6

Mingyur Rinpoche's Story

To make the topic of dissolution a little less esoteric, I'd like to tell a story about someone who actually *was* prepared, through study and practice, to recognize and experience the dissolution process during a near-death experience. This is a story recounted by Yongey Mingyur Rinpoche in his book *In Love with the World: A Monk's Journey through the Bardos of Living and Dying*.

Mingyur Rinpoche, a very popular teacher from an illustrious family of Tibetan teachers, was the abbot of a monastery in Bodhgaya, India, the place where the Buddha attained enlightenment. For the first thirty-six years of his life, he had been sheltered and privileged. In childhood, he was identified as a *tulku*, a reincarnation of a previous enlightened teacher. His father, the great meditation master Tulku Urgyen Rinpoche, brought him up as both son and student. At home in Nepal, his parents showered him with love and affection and never let him go anywhere by himself. Even after he left home to begin his formal studies, he was always protected by his role and status. This continued into adulthood. Before age thirty-six, he had never been alone outside in his entire life.

Then, in June 2011, he got up in the middle of the night and left the monastery to embark on a wandering retreat that would last over four years. He had done many retreats in the past, including one for three years, but they had all taken place at monasteries or hermitages. The wandering retreat had been a dream of his from a young age; he had long been inspired by stories of ascetics living freely and spontaneously, taking whatever food or shelter might come their way.

All he had with him were two Buddhist texts, a small amount of money, and the clothes he was wearing. No one knew he was leaving. When his attendant came into his room the following afternoon, he found a farewell letter in which Mingyur Rinpoche expressed his wish to follow the examples of the wandering yogis of the past such as Milarepa, who spent most of his life meditating in remote caves and sacred sites. And to continue to guide his students, Mingyur Rinpoche had left a well-organized course of study using simple meditation instructions along with hundreds of hours of recorded teachings.

Before he left the monastery, his vision for the retreat had a touch of the romantic: caves and beautiful lakes and pleasant train rides. His only plan was to take the first train to Varanasi, the ancient city on the Ganges where Hindus and Buddhists have done spiritual practice for millennia. But first he had to figure out how to buy a train ticket because he'd never done that before. Then, when he got on the train in the cheapest compartment, his overwhelming experience was aversion. It was incredibly crowded; everyone smelled bad and looked bad; he could see lice in people's hair. No one paid any respect to his Buddhist robes; he got pushed and shoved just like everyone else.

But he kept saying to himself that this was what he wanted: to have everything fall apart and to have his normal way of being not work at all. He wanted to test his practice in the middle of all this. And what's so inspiring to me is that he didn't just cruise through his experience. He was overcome with fear and aversion, just as you and I would be. He used every practice he'd ever been given, not caring if it was "beginning" or "advanced." In whatever situation that came up, he did everything he could to stay present and work with his mind, even if he felt disgusted or afraid to the point where he almost couldn't bear it.

Not too long after that train ride, he went to Kushinagar, the place where the Buddha passed away. He spent most of his time meditating in a park commemorating the Buddha's death. For a little while, he had money to stay in a guesthouse and buy street food. But when that ran out, he had to start sleeping outside and begging. During this transition, he stopped wearing his maroon Buddhist robes and began wearing the saffron robes of a sadhu, a Hindu renunciant. He considered this change to be an important part of going forward into the unknown. The Buddhist robes had always sheltered him and given him a sense of identity, and he wanted to go beyond all his usual reference points—with nothing to hold on to and nothing to hide behind.

Begging was very hard for him. It pushed against everything in his being to have to go up to someone and ask for food. The first place he begged was at a food stall he'd been going to regularly. The manager noticed his change of clothes and said, "You are Hindu now!" Then the manager matter-of-factly told him to come back in the evening, when they put out all the food scraped from plates for the beggars. He spent much of the day meditating on his embarrassment, using the teachings to work with that emotion, and by the time he returned to the stall, he was ready to accept the leftovers. He was so hungry that he said he enjoyed that meal more than anything he'd ever eaten at a five-star hotel.

His first night sleeping outside was near the Cremation Stupa, a large mound of dirt containing the relics from the Buddha's cremation. He couldn't sleep because of the mosquitoes and toward morning he developed stomach cramps. When he was meditating the next day, he started having diarrhea and by evening he was vomiting.

As things got worse over the next few days, he realized he was dying. The first sign he recognized was the earth element dissolving into water. He began to feel so heavy it seemed his weight might push him below the surface of the earth. As another sign of this dissolution, his vision became blurry. Then he felt around his mouth with his tongue and there was no saliva. Though he was too dehydrated for fluids to be leaving his body, he understood that the water element was dissolving. Now he thought, "It's happening. This is my big chance." (Can you imagine having such a fearless attitude?) Then he became very cold, and since the air outside was extremely hot, he took this as an unmistakable sign of the fire element dissolving. Then, as the air element dissolved into consciousness, he felt like he was being inflated like a balloon every time he inhaled.

He still had a sense of himself as an individual person going through an experience. There was still a feeling of "Mingyur Rinpoche" observing and tracking what was happening. But, as he described it, his conceptual mind was "draining away." And at the same time his true nature was becoming more and more vivid. Then, at one point, he almost blacked out, and flashes of white and red appeared before his mind.

What occurred next was beyond anything he had ever experienced. After the fact, he found it nearly impossible to describe it in words, but his book gives you the flavor of it. There was still a bright awareness, but it was not conceptual in any way. There was no self and other, no inside and outside, no time, no direction, no life, no death. And at the same time, everything was made of love. The trees, the stars, the entire world was made of love.

Before this experience, he had spent a great deal of time meditating on the sky-like nature of his mind, so to some extent he was prepared. His years of training enabled him to understand what was happening. But his recognition of his mind's nature had never been so complete.

Later, he guessed he was in this state for about five hours. He knows it was dark when he entered this non-conceptual phase and light when he came to. But this "coming to" didn't happen in the ordinary way of someone passing out and then recovering consciousness. If someone else had seen him, they probably would have thought he'd passed out, but in a deeper sense, he was awake the whole time—awake to cloudless awareness, to the universal open mind.

Eventually, he did come back to his body. This wasn't a decision he made; there was no sense of "I" involved. But somehow a movement of mind occurred, based on recognizing his work as a teacher wasn't done.

He felt himself reentering his body. His normal breath returned and his body warmed up. When he opened his eyes, everything appeared transformed. He said the trees were green as usual, but they were shining. He was still very dehydrated, so he got up to go to the water pump. Then he really did pass out, and when he awoke he was in a hospital with an IV in his arm. (How he got there is a whole other fascinating story, which is in Mingyur Rinpoche's book.)

So this is a story of someone actually going through the process of the elements dissolving and experiencing the clouds parting to reveal the wide-open infinite sky of his mind. Mingyur Rinpoche, of course, came back, so he couldn't tell us what would have happened next had he stayed. But as it is, this story illustrates the power and importance of continually training in staying open and in familiarizing ourselves with the everlasting in-betweenness of life.

From the night he left the monastery and through every experience he had over the next four years, he tried to live fully in the wondrous flow of birth and death. His near-death experience was just one part of that flow, and as soon as he was well enough (which was before the doctor thought he was well enough), he ventured back out into the complete unknown, with no security other than his big-sky mind. For me, nothing about the practice of Dharma is more inspiring than seeing how it leads to such fearlessness.

7

Mother and Child Luminosity

A traditional way of describing the final dissolution of this life—consciousness dissolving into space—is in terms of the "child luminosity" meeting the "mother luminosity." The child luminosity is the experience of our mind's sky-like nature, with which we can familiarize ourselves through training. In the Tibetan Buddhist tradition, a teacher points out this nature to a student and gives the student instructions on how to cultivate and stabilize the experience of wide-open, unfettered mind. These teachings and practices are all designed to develop confidence in the child luminosity. This is how Mingyur Rinpoche had spent many years of his life, and this was why he was so prepared to die.

The mother luminosity—also known as the "ground luminosity"—is the ultimate nature of reality, which is no different from our own nature. It's the infinitely open space of awareness that encompasses everything and everyone. It's the basic goodness of the universe, imbued with compassion and wisdom. And what I find so inspiring is that people like you and me can always connect with it. Yet, although it's continually present, it is only fully and completely revealed to us at the end of the dissolution process—and only then if we recognize it.

When we've prepared ourselves well by training in the child luminosity, we will recognize our mother when she shows her face. Then, like a small child who has been with a babysitter all day, we will naturally run to our mother to become reunited with her. As it says in one of the prayers about the bardos that I often recite: "May I be liberated, as naturally as a child running to its mother's lap."

The child luminosity can be compared to the space inside a vase and the mother luminosity to the larger space outside. Though the inner and outer spaces are separated by the vase and we can talk about them as if they're two different spaces, their essence is exactly the same. Both are simply space. When the vase breaks—analogous to death—the barrier between the two spaces disappears and they merge into one.

When we use the term "luminosity" to talk about our mind's nature, we're not talking about something like ordinary light. Luminosity is the quality of our mind that is aware. It is that which knows. It's how we know what we're seeing and hearing and thinking and feeling, and it's how we have the potential to know our own true nature. Maybe it's more helpful simply to call it "open awareness," something we can practice and connect with.

If we familiarize ourselves with the continuous flow of births and deaths, the continuous bardos that make up our life, we can gradually over time come to see that this awareness is the background of every experience. We can get to the point where open awareness accompanies us through every beginning and every ending, through every up and every down. It doesn't appear and disappear. It's there in all the transitions and gaps. It's a permanent feature of our mind's landscape. This may seem far off right now, but it's our birthright, an always beckoning possibility.

When we try to locate, describe, or conceptualize this open awareness in any way, we can't. However hard we search, we can find nothing to pin down. And yet it's possible to get to know this awareness so intimately that we will always be able to recognize it, in every situation that arises, even during the dissolution of our body. This, of course, is the most important time of all.

Most of the time we're too caught up to be aware of this openness—caught up in our thoughts and emotions, in our hopes and fears, in our general resistance to things as they are. In the traditional analogy, we are like a desperately poor person who worries and struggles day and night, but doesn't realize that right under their house is an enormous cache of gold that would instantly free them from poverty.

The Buddha and other great teachers have taught many methods for uncovering our luminous mind. When Trungpa Rinpoche first taught meditation in the West, he asked his students to relax and simply rest undistractedly in the present. If thoughts carried them away, they were to return again to the present moment. When this turned out to be nearly impossible for most people, he introduced relating to the out-breath as an object, but with a light touch. "Touch the breath as it goes out, and let it go"—these were the instructions I first learned.

The most commonly taught techniques involve sitting in a meditation posture, focusing on an object such as the breath, and having a technique for working with thoughts when they arise. This and most other Buddhist practices, in one way or another, involve slowing down the mind enough to see our habitual thought patterns and how they usually take up almost all our attention. These methods ventilate our tendency to be totally engrossed in our thoughts, so we can touch in, over and over, with the sky behind the clouds.*

One simple method for doing this I call the pause practice. You just stop whatever you're doing and look out. You could do this almost any time. You're walking around or washing dishes, and then you pause and look out. The pause interrupts the momentum of being completely caught up in thoughts. Instead you enjoy a glimpse of freshness, of what Trungpa Rinpoche called "nowness." It may not be a full experience of nowness, but this glimpse teaches you about the contrast between being caught up and being open. You're getting a glimpse of your true nature. You're starting to have a sense of what it is.

Once when I was teaching on this topic, someone asked me, "Will this get clearer and more obvious with time?" She said that even though she'd heard these teachings and done a fair amount of meditation, she didn't have a real sense of what was meant by words like "open awareness" and "sky-like mind." She guessed it was because she was too conceptually oriented, always trying to figure things out.

I thought about her question for a moment and then I said, "Whether it gets more clear will always be up to you." Getting to know open awareness doesn't usually happen by itself. It's a process. Many people have spent years learning to relax enough to become intimate with

* For instructions on basic sitting meditation and meditating with open awareness, see appendix B (pages 181–87).

their sky-like mind. If any of us are really curious about the wide-open space behind our habitual thought patterns, if we want to know the sky behind the clouds intimately, then it will take devoting time to the endeavor.

But before we begin, we should know that this isn't a project of making our thoughts into an enemy. Clouds come and go without harming the sky. Like that, thoughts come and go without harming our mind. Whether we like it or not, the thoughts keep coming. That's just how things are. We don't have to see it as a problem. So instead of demonizing our thoughts, a more gentle and productive approach is simple curiosity. We can simply wonder: *What's behind this whole thing if I'm suddenly not thinking? What will I experience? What are these thoughts, anyway? Are they really solid? Are they really a threat?*

If you have this kind of curiosity, you'll naturally look into the situation more. You'll study and practice and the experience will become clearer. More and more often, you'll remember to pause and interrupt the onrush of your thoughts. The thoughts you have will gradually become less problematic. More and more often, you'll enjoy moments of freshness and spaciousness. And the more you commit to this kind of inquisitiveness, the clearer and more obvious your sense of open awareness becomes.

The first time I ever had a distinct experience of my mind's openness came about in a humorous way. It was the day I discovered the gap. I was at a long retreat where we sat in a meditation hall every day, all day. There was a loud fan in the room, but after a short time I was so used to it that I stopped noticing it. I was feeling poverty-stricken. We had received teachings on our mind's nature, and people kept talking about the "gap" and "spaciousness," and

I didn't know what they were talking about. It got to the point where this felt like my dark little secret. So I was thinking along these depressing lines—and all of a sudden the fan shut off for about three seconds and then came back on. And I knew: *That's it!* The "gap," the "spaciousness"—whatever you want to call it—was right there. There was the fan's hum, then no sound: a gap. It was as if someone pushed pause on my experience. Then the hum began again. Although there was nothing I could directly put my finger on, I recognized that the open space had always been right here. It was a revelation because it was so simple.

It may seem like I had this experience just because the fan shut off, but I've been in lots of situations where a fan shut off and I continued plodding along in my train of thought. But it only happened because I was there in the meditation hall, badly wanting to know, and doing my best to follow the instructions. In retrospect, the whole time I was feeling like a loser who couldn't do anything right, I was actually laying the groundwork for this experience of recognition to happen.

Training our mind to recognize open awareness is a long-term exploration of working with our deeply ingrained habits. We're so used to being caught up in our struggle against life as it is that we often turn our practice into another form of struggle. If we take up this endeavor, we may find ourselves often wondering what we're doing and doubting ourselves. We're all good at finding ways of tying ourselves in knots. But if we continue to be curious and to apply the instructions we've been given, our mind's true nature becomes increasingly familiar. We come to know who we really are behind the kaleidoscope of perceptions and thoughts that make up our experience. Then we'll be prepared for whatever may happen to us—even experiences of groundlessness that would normally be deeply unsettling. Finally, when the elements of our body dissolve, we will have the deep joy and solace of a child recognizing their mother and running without hesitation into her comforting lap.

8

What Goes through
the Bardos?

When we talk about death happening every moment, we also might have a natural question: "If I'm continuously being born and dying, then who is it that goes through all these experiences?" Once this body is dead, who has the chance to merge with the mother luminosity? If that chance is missed, who goes on to the next bardo, known as "the bardo of dharmata"? When it comes to reincarnation, who gets reborn? A similar question would be "What is it that continues from lifetime to lifetime?" Or "What goes through the bardos?"

The standard answer to all these questions is "consciousness," or *namshé* in Tibetan. The word "consciousness" could mean different things to different people, but the Tibetan language is extremely precise when it comes to describing the mind. *Namshé* implies that this consciousness is dualistic. For instance, if Rosa sees a mountain, Rosa is here and the mountain is there: they are two separate things. Whatever Rosa sees, hears, smells, tastes, or feels seems like an object separate from Rosa.

This is how things appear to all of us, right? There's a sense of a division between me and everything else. The experiences keep changing, but I always seem to remain the same. There's something about me that feels like it never changes. But when I look for this unchanging me, I find that I can't pin anything down.

I was born on July 14, 1936. My name at that time was Deirdre Blomfield-Brown. I can definitely acknowledge there's a connection between that infant Deirdre and today's Pema. I have memories of my childhood. The mother and father I had then are still my mother and father to me, even though they're long gone. A scientist would say that the baby and I have the same DNA. And of course we have the same birthday. But the interesting question remains: Are the newborn baby and the elderly woman I am today actually the same person?

I still have pictures of myself as an infant and a toddler. If I try hard, I can pick out some ways that child looks similar to what I see today in the mirror. But I also know intellectually that not a single cell of my body has stayed the same. Even at present, every cell and every atom of my body is continuously changing.

I've tried long and hard to find a real me that stays the same from year to year—or even from moment to moment—but I've never had any success. (This is a worthwhile exercise, which I highly recommend to anyone interested in the mysteries of life and death.) So where does this leave us in terms of the bardos?

As I said, the standard answer for what continues across lifetimes is *namshé*, dualistic consciousness. This is not so easy to understand. A while ago, I called my friend Ken McLeod, a highly learned Buddhist practitioner who's written some of my favorite books, and I asked him about it. Like other students of the Dharma, he said that *namshé* is what goes through the bardos. But he made the point that this consciousness isn't some stable entity that flows through everything. It's constantly dissolving and reforming. Every moment, we experience something new: the smell of toast, a change of light, a thought about a friend. And every moment we have a sense of a self having that experience—a sense of "I, the smeller of toast." When this moment passes, it's immediately followed by another moment with a subject and an object. This flow of dualistic experience continues uninterruptedly through our waking hours and our dreams, through this life and across lifetimes.

But beyond this flow of moments, is there anything underlying them all that we could point to as "consciousness"? We can't locate or describe any stable element that lives through all our experiences. So from this point of view, Ken said that another answer to "What goes through the bardos?" is "Nothing." There are just individual moments, happening one after another. What we think of as "consciousness" is fluid, more like a verb than a noun.

When Ken and I had this conversation, it gave me a better feeling for how I keep clinging to this self as something permanent, when it's actually much more dynamic than that. It's not some fixed, frozen thing. We can have this view of ourselves as frozen—and we can have frozen opinions of others as well—but that's just based on a misunderstanding.

Why do we have this misunderstanding? Who can say? It's just how we've always seen things. The Buddhist term for it is "co-emergent ignorance," or, as Anam Thubten calls it, "co-emergent unawareness." We all come into our life with this unawareness. And what are we unaware of? We are unaware that we are not a solid, permanent entity, and that we are not separate from what we perceive. This is the big misunderstanding, the illusion of separateness.

Here is how I've heard teachers talk about the origin of our unawareness. First, there is open space, fluid and dynamic. There is no sense of duality, no sense of "me" separate from everything else. Then, from that ground, everything becomes manifest. If properly understood, the open space and the manifestation are not two separate things. They are like the sun and its rays. This means that everything we're experiencing right now is a display of our own mind. Recognizing this union is called "co-emergent wisdom" or "co-emergent awareness." Remaining caught in the illusion of separateness and solidity is co-emergent unawareness.

And this, of course, is where you and I find ourselves. It's obvious that co-emergent unawareness is our usual experience. But in reality, no one and no thing in our world is fixed and static. Consciousness is a process that constantly dissolves and reforms, both now and in the bardo. And every time it reforms, it's completely fresh and new—which means that we have an endless stream of opportunities to have a completely fresh, open take. We always have another chance to see the world anew, a chance to reconnect with basic openness, a chance to realize we've never been separate from that basic spaciousness—a chance to realize it's all just been a big misunderstanding.

If you spend enough time pondering this, you might understand it with your rational mind. But then you may still ask yourself, "Why do I experience myself as separate? Why don't I experience each moment as fresh? Why do I feel so stuck?" The reason you feel this way is because you—like everyone else—have been under the sway of co-emergent unawareness for a very, very long time. Therefore, it takes a very, very long time to dismantle.

Our misunderstanding of separateness goes deep. Even animals have an innate sense of being a separate entity. But unlike animals, we have the ability to contemplate. We can use our fairly sophisticated brains to realize that our misunderstanding is indeed a misunderstanding— that moment by moment, we have a chance, even if briefly, to merge with that basic ground again.

Even if we're convinced of this, however, we can't drop our familiar sense of separateness just by willing it to go away. But what we can do is start to meditate. In one session on our meditation cushion, we can see for ourselves how fluid our consciousness is. We can observe how our thoughts and emotions and perceptions appear and disappear, and how this process just goes on and on without a break.

We can also see how mysterious our thoughts are. Where do all those thoughts come from? And where do they go? And why do we get so serious about what goes on in our mind? Even though our thoughts are as elusive as mist, how can they cause us endless unnecessary problems? How can they make us worry, get jealous, quarrel with others, get euphoric and depressed?

Meditation gives us a way to see the slipperiness of our mind and of our notion of "me." When we practice meditation, we gradually accustom ourselves to how experiences constantly flow. We see that this happens even though we can't pinpoint any subject who experiences them.

From this point of view, there is no fixed being who goes through the bardos. Another way of saying this is there's no continuous individual who experiences life and death. No one lives and no one dies. Life and death, beginnings and endings, gains and losses are like dreams or magical illusions.

9

The Two Truths

In the Buddhist teachings, there's an idea that everything has two levels of truth, relative and absolute: how we experience life when we're immersed in it, and how we experience it from a distance when we can get a vaster perspective.

I like to think of the relative truth as what goes into the story of an ordinary day: what we see and hear and think, how we feel about the people and objects we encounter, how we relate to our world, how things appear and function.

Trees grow up from the ground, they have branches and leaves, and many of them lose their leaves in the fall. These statements are "truth" because everyone agrees to them. There's a consensus reality that we agree on. If someone says, "Trees grow downward from the sky," we say they're not speaking the truth because that isn't the consensus reality. For human beings, the existence of trees is an agreed-upon relative truth. But we can guess that termites have no sense of "tree." They see the same thing in terms of what it means to them—as food and a place to live. So something as uncontroversial as a tree really depends on who's looking at it, when they're looking at it, how closely they're looking, and what they're interested in seeing.

This is true about everything in the universe. Our relative world is more tentative and open to interpretation than we generally give it credit for being. This is where relative and absolute come together. When we perceive something without our usual concepts, we discover *shunyata*, or "emptiness," an often-misunderstood word. Emptiness doesn't refer to a void: it doesn't suggest a cold, dark world in which nothing has any meaning. What it means is that everything we examine is free from—"empty" of—our conceptual interpretation, our views and opinions. Nothing in this world is fixed; nothing is permanently and definitively one way or another. All phenomena are just as they are, free of our value judgments and preconceptions.

I see a mouse and think, "Cute." Another person feels fear. Another gets aggressive, so watch out, little mouse! But the mouse isn't inherently any of these things. Despite all our ideas and opinions about this small creature, mouse just remains mouse, just as it is, free of our conceptual overlays.

"Absolute truth" refers to this open, unpinpointable nature of the world and everything in it: ourselves, other living beings, our environment, everything. It's called "absolute" because it doesn't depend on anything else to be true. It's just the nature of how things are. When we can take a step back and simply relax with this absolute truth, we will be far less inclined to insist that life has to be on our terms and far more inclined to think of how our actions affect the whole.

When the astronaut Edgar Mitchell walked on the moon in 1971 and saw the Earth from that vast perspective, he realized that it was just one Earth and that all the divisions humans had created—divisions that caused so much pain—were arbitrary and meaningless. He realized that we Earthlings had to work together and that separateness was an illusion. "From out there on the moon," he said, "international politics looks so petty." Mitchell had an absolute experience of how things really are. When he returned home, this perspective continued to affect how he lived. Yet he still had to relate with the relative world and how it triggered his propensities and caused him to put up barriers between himself and others—the very same pain-causing barriers that from space he had seen as meaningless.

When I was very young, I had an experience of the absolute that was so straightforward it might be helpful to share it here. One summer night, I was lying on my back, looking up at the stars, as I had done many times. Like so many others throughout time I was enthralled by the feeling it gave me to gaze up at all those stars. On this particular evening, however, something shifted for me and I had one of those light-bulb experiences. I suddenly knew, without really thinking about it, that this was the same vast space that children in ancient Greece had experienced, that prehistoric people had experienced. I knew that before I was born it had been here, and that after I died it would be here. For years, this was my own personal secret, something I didn't want to spoil by talking about it.

Seeing the stars was a relative experience happening on a New Jersey night in 1943. The sure understanding that this space had always been there, and would always be there, was an absolute, timeless experience.

The word "absolute" sounds more impressive than "relative," but we don't need to think one truth is superior to the other. We can fully experience a tree's beauty without thinking that our way of looking at the tree is *the* way to look at it. We can enjoy its shade on a hot day while knowing that it is far more mysterious than we generally assume. Our aim on the spiritual path is not to get rid of the relative and dwell in emptiness. The two truths go hand in hand.

The terms "relative" and "absolute" give us ways to talk about the same subject from two different angles. When we say that nothing goes through the bardos, we're speaking from a bigger perspective, from the absolute point of view. The consciousness that runs through all our moments and bridges the gap between lifetimes is constantly dissolving and reforming. Try as we might, we can never find anything to put our finger on.

In the absolute, no one lives, no one dies, and no one goes through the bardos. But in the relative, when a loved one passes we grieve. From the relative point of view, we experience pain and pleasure, hope and fear, thoughts and perceptions, life and death. From the relative perspective, everything we do affects ourselves and our world, and everything we do matters.

Our actions always have consequences. Padmasambhava—commonly known as Guru Rinpoche—the eighth-century Indian teacher who established Buddhism in Tibet, said, "My view is higher than the sky, but my attention to my actions and their effects is finer than flour." Even though he was an enlightened master, he knew how crucial it was to pay attention to the relative details of his life and the consequences of his actions.

The Buddha didn't teach his disciples so they would end up in some frigid, intellectual realm divorced from day-to-day experience. On the contrary, he gave many teachings on how we should conduct ourselves in ways that will bring ourselves and others joy and relief from pain. These teachings include profound, concrete advice on how to live our lives and how to approach death. They are based on the two truths: the understanding that, although nothing is really happening on the ultimate level, we would all rather experience happiness than suffering.

10

———

Propensities

Before going any further in describing the journey after death and the experiences of the next bardos, I think it's important to take a pause and present some words from the heart about how to work with our mind, our emotions, and our propensities. Why is that? It's because how we work with our mind, emotions, and propensities while journeying through the ups and downs of the bardo of this life is what we'll take with us as we travel forward. They say, "You can't take it with you," but when it comes to our state of mind and our emotional patterns, we *do* take them with us. And just as our thoughts and emotions create our experience of the world right now, in that same way, and even more intensely, they will create the environment we find ourselves in after death. If you want to experience heaven, work with your thoughts and emotions. If you want to avoid hell, work with your thoughts and emotions. It's like that. Therefore, in the next several chapters, I will give some practice instructions on how to connect skillfully and compassionately with our habitual patterns and emotions.

When Trungpa Rinpoche was asked what goes through the bardos, he answered with a big smile, "All your bad habits." I took this to mean that whatever habits I hadn't befriended and let go of in this life would travel forward through the intermediate state, to be passed on to some poor infant in the future.

Back in the seventies, when my son and daughter were teenagers, I took them and their friend to meet His Holiness the Sixteenth Karmapa, one of the teachers who meant the most to me. My children aren't Buddhist, but they've always been friendly in relation to the Dharma and they were willing to humor their enthusiastic mother. His Holiness didn't speak English, so we communicated through an interpreter. I asked the Karmapa if he could speak to the children and he started giving them a little teaching on Buddhism. When he paused after a little while, I told him respectfully that the children weren't Buddhist and I asked if he could say something that would be meaningful to them despite their lack of background.

His Holiness the Karmapa was a big, awe-inspiring man and we were sitting quite close to him. He looked at the three teenagers intensely and said, "You are going to die." Then he added, "And you won't take anything with you but your state of mind."

What Trungpa Rinpoche said about bad habits was a relative teaching about what goes through the bardos. Ken McLeod's comments that actually nothing goes through the bardos are from an absolute point of view. The Karmapa's words to the teenagers were a little bit of both—for what exactly did he mean by "your state of mind"?

These words sound like they describe something static, but as I've said, our state of mind is always changing. We continuously go from one state of mind to another. There is only this flow of mind—a mindstream. Nevertheless, our mindstream follows a certain course, which is not random. Its course is determined by our habits, our tendencies, our propensities. What does this mean?

In the Buddha's teachings on karma, the teachings on cause and effect, whatever we do, say, or even think makes an imprint in our mind. When we do something once, we're likely to do it again. When we react to a situation in a certain way, we're likely to react the same way next time that situation comes up. This is how propensities develop. As a result, we usually behave and react predictably. In some particular circumstances, we're very generous; in others we're self-protective. In some, we're tolerant; in others, irritable. In some, confident; in others, insecure. And every time we react in our habitual ways, we strengthen our propensities. This is similar to the findings in neuroscience that show how pathways in our brain get reinforced by our habitual actions and thinking patterns.

Say you have a propensity to feel inadequate, especially about your work. You're in the office talking to two co-workers and your supervisor barges in and says, "You people did a lousy job." The supervisor is actually criticizing all three of you, but you're the one with the strong propensity to take it personally, so you feel totally wretched, as if it's all your fault. There's already a long history behind your propensity, and the supervisor's comment seems to add to the evidence against you. Now you go into a familiar storyline: "I never get it right. I'm worthless. I'm hopeless. I always blow it." You experience yourself as a loser. And beneath all these concepts is a horribly unpleasant emotion that you would do anything to get rid of.

In this scenario, it might seem like the cause of your suffering is your supervisor's words. However, the words are only the trigger. The actual cause is your preexisting propensity. It's important to mention here that the point of saying this isn't to blame the victim. All three of you agree that the supervisor's words were mean-spirited and insensitive. But at the same time, it's important to see the full picture of what's going on. Your propensity to feel inadequate was already a recurring theme in your life. Hearing "You did a lousy job" was the trigger that provided the right conditions for it to fully emerge. It's like a crocus bulb that lies dormant under the earth for much of the year and in the spring, with the right causes and conditions, suddenly comes out as a brilliant flower.

In this example, the other two people receiving criticism have completely different experiences because of their own propensities. One of them has the propensity to get furious and take action, so he marches off to the supervisor in a towering rage, prints up some banners, and gets a whole gang of people to sign a petition.

The third person doesn't get triggered in any defensive way, but she still acts based on her own propensity. Her go-to response in any uncomfortable work situation is to become the peacemaker. So she acknowledges that the supervisor's speech was unskillful and encourages the whole group to take part in a workshop on effective and nonviolent communication.

When I look back on what the Karmapa told my children, I now think he meant something along these lines: "When you die, all that you'll take with you is your propensities." And with that came some powerful unspoken advice: "So you better take good care of your propensities now, while you still have time."

We already have ample experience with the trouble our propensities cause in our current lifetime. Our unhelpful thought patterns and self-destructive emotional habits have undermined us repeatedly. Not only do our propensities disturb us internally, but they also manifest as difficult outer situations. Some people always have a problem with their boss. No matter how many times they change jobs, they consistently find themselves in the same uncomfortable situations. Some people have problems with intimacy in relationships. No matter who they date, their intimacy issue persists. The actors change, the movie set changes, but the basic drama remains the same. This is because our propensities are the authors of the script.

Another thing about these propensities is that they don't stop by themselves. We have to recognize them when they arise and not be so predictable. Over and over again we have to find our way to do something different. If not, they will follow us for the rest of our life. We can go even further and say they'll follow us beyond this life— through the bardos and into our next life, writing scene after scene after scene. They will create the outer and inner circumstances of our next moment, our next day, our next life, and all our lives to come.

The other side of the coin is that, because of the strong interconnected relationship between our mind and our world, we will often find that changing our mental and emotional habits has a powerful effect on our outer experience. It seems like a miracle, but it's quite simple and straightforward if you think about it. If you work with your propensity to get jealous, it will seem like there are fewer and fewer people to envy. If you work with your anger, people won't make you so mad.

So how do we "take good care of our propensities"? We get to know them with kindness and intelligence. We acknowledge how powerful they are, but we don't make them the enemy. One of my teachers, Tsoknyi Rinpoche, calls them our "beautiful monsters" and advises us to treat them with tenderness—not acting them out or repressing them, but making friends with them just as they are. Then, when a person or an event triggers our painful emotions, we can distinguish between the trigger and the propensity. We can ask ourselves, as openly and objectively as possible, "What is the main cause of my suffering? Is it my supervisor or is it my propensities?" This kind of closeness and friendship with our propensities creates the right causes and conditions for them to loosen up and unwind.

For instance, you've been getting into a lot of arguments with your partner and now you see them laughing and smiling with another person. Immediately the pain of jealousy arises in your heart. But instead of habitually reacting to that jealousy, say by getting drunk or speaking in a passive-aggressive way, you can ask yourself, "What is the cause of my pain? Is it the laughing and smiling, or is it my preexisting propensity to get jealous?" Then you can check in with your body and get in touch with that propensity. How does it feel? Is it tight or loose, contracted or expansive? Does it have a temperature, a color, a special quality? If you investigate the unpleasant feeling of jealousy with mindfulness and gentleness, you will learn much about it. You will see your history with it. You will start to notice patterns. You will see that this feeling often arises in your life, and that you tend to make a mess when it does. This could be the beginning of your taking care of the propensity. This could be the beginning of seeing that your propensities are just fluid sensations having nothing to do with good or bad.

Once you've learned something through this process, you could, of course, go in less helpful directions. You could simply go on with your usual way of doing things, as unaffected by your self-reflection as if you just learned some unimportant fact about a subject that doesn't mean much to you. Even worse, you could use your self-knowledge to beat yourself up: "I have this terrible propensity, which makes me a terrible person. Even though I'm embarrassed to behave like this, I'm doomed to continue acting out of jealousy for the rest of my life."

Neither of these options will do anything to help us make friends with our beautiful monsters. We will keep thinking and acting in the same ways, strengthening our propensities and making ourselves unnecessarily miserable. It will be like finding undesirable seeds in our garden and giving them more water and nutrients to grow.

The most helpful alternative is to look objectively at what is happening and try to learn something from it, something that will enable us to see clearly how to proceed. This way of working with our propensities in our daily life will definitely pay off when we die. Before death, when actually dying, and beyond that, people predictably experience a wide range of strong emotions, and how we relate to them is important.

11

Feel What You Feel

Is death an enemy or a friend?
That, my dear, depends on you.

I saw this quote written on a wall in San Francisco and it stopped my mind. Of course, whether old age, illness, or death are our friends or enemies is entirely up to us. It all depends on how our mind is set. And, to a large extent, it depends on how we work with our emotions. So, how do you, right now, work with your emotions? This is worth looking into. Knowing how to work with our emotions is really the key to finding balance and equanimity, qualities that support us as we go forward through all the transitions and gaps that we are yet to experience.

One of the most famous slogans from the popular Buddhist text *The Seven Points of Mind Training* is "Drive all blames into one." When I began to study this slogan, I had a sense of the basic idea: it may seem like outer circumstances are provoking us and making us suffer, but the real culprit is always our own ego-clinging. But for many years, I found it difficult to apply this teaching in a personal way. First of all, I wasn't quite sure what they meant by "ego-clinging." It seemed like an abstract concept and I didn't know how to relate it to my own experience. I also had trouble with the idea of "blame." To me it sounded like I should blame myself, which was what I tended to do anyway. I knew that wasn't the intent of the teaching, but I wasn't sure how else to interpret it.

Then I heard a talk by Dzigar Kongtrul Rinpoche in which he used the phrase "the propensity to be bothered," and something clicked for me. Though he wasn't speaking directly about "Drive all blames into one," I began to understand how this slogan is a teaching on propensities. While ego-clinging seemed abstract and conceptual, how we experience ego-clinging—our propensities—was something I knew intimately on a daily basis. The slogan was encouraging me to recognize my propensities, my beautiful monsters, as the cause of unnecessary unhappiness.

The Dharma tells us that all our experiences of discomfort, anxiety, being disturbed, and being bothered are rooted in our *kleshas*. This Sanskrit term means "destructive emotions" or "pain-causing emotions." The three main kleshas are craving, aggression, and ignorance. The first two don't require much explanation. "Craving" becomes a destructive emotion when it gets to the point of being an addiction or an obsession. I was once given some Asian candy whose brand name was "Baby Want-Want." That sums up craving quite nicely, I think. We think something will bring us pleasure or comfort, so we become obsessed with having it or keeping it. "Aggression" is the opposite: we want to get rid of something that we perceive as a threat to our well-being. "Ignorance" as a destructive emotion is a little harder to understand. It's a dull, indifferent state of mind that actually contains a deep level of pain. It can express itself as being out of touch, being mentally lethargic, not caring what we're feeling or what others are going through. When this state of mind dominates us, it can turn into depression.

These three kleshas are often called the "three poisons" because, as Anam Thubten says, they kill our happiness. This often happens to us in two ways. First, we suffer while we experience anger, addiction, depression, jealousy, and the rest; then we continue to suffer as a result of the harmful actions they provoke.

You probably have firsthand experience of being unhappy when these poisons arise in your life. But how exactly do they kill your happiness? According to the Buddha's teachings, it's not the emotions themselves that make us suffer. In their raw form—before we start to struggle with them and before our thinking process gets involved—they are just sensations or forms of energy. They are not intrinsically bad or good. This is important to remember. The destructive aspect of aggression, for instance, is not the sensation; it's our rejection of that sensation and what we then do as a response. The culprit isn't the basic energy but the spin-off, what the Buddhist teacher Sharon Salzberg calls "the add-ons."

When klesha energy arises, we tend to react in one of a few ways. One is to act out—either physically or with our words. Another is to suppress the emotion, to go numb around it; this may involve diverting our attention elsewhere, say by zoning out with Netflix. A third common reaction is to get mentally wrapped up in some kind of storyline, one that often involves blame. All these reactions are based on our not being able to bear the discomfort of the energy. We have a propensity to be bothered by this energy, so we try to escape our discomfort by getting rid of what's causing it. This approach is similar to that of the tyrant who kills the messenger bringing bad news instead of relating to the message. But when we indulge in any of these reactions, we only strengthen our pain-causing habits and perpetuate our misery in the long run. Somehow this is a hard lesson to learn.

Everyone has these habits. There's no need to blame ourselves or anyone else for this process. Instead of blaming or feeling helpless, we can apply time-tested methods for working with our emotions constructively. Like everything else in the universe, the kleshas and our reactions to them are impermanent and insubstantial. This is what makes it possible for us to change our habits.

In general, lack of awareness is what gives our emotions their power. Bringing awareness to them is the magic key. When we're aware of what's happening, they lose their ability to make us miserable.

The first step in every method of working with emotions is simply to recognize what's happening. One of the characteristics of the kleshas is that they tend to go undetected. We only notice them when they've become full-blown. We're unaware of the emotion while it's just an ember; by the time we smell the burning or feel the fire's heat, it's too late. We've struck out in words or actions, or we're already on a binge.

Here is a fairly common example of the life cycle of a klesha. You catch a glimpse of someone in the hallway, someone you have issues with. You experience a faint tension in your shoulders or a subtle tug in your chest. This is the ember stage. Next thing you know, you're having judgmental or resentful thoughts about the person. This stage is like when logs in a wood stove have caught fire.

There's a lot more heat than at the ember stage, but at least it's still contained. Even this level may go unnoticed. But if you keep unconsciously escalating your storyline, it's as if you're pouring kerosene on the fire. Eventually it will be too much for the stove to contain and it might even burn down your house. At that point, you and everyone else will notice, but it will be too late to prevent a great deal of unavoidable pain. The damaging text message has been written, you've already pressed "Send," and there's no way to take it back.

Even then, there are ways of making the situation better and ways of making it worse. At every moment, and in every bardo experience, we have these two basic alternatives. We can escalate or deescalate our misery. We can strengthen unhelpful habits or ventilate them. By becoming more conscious of what's happening, we can put out the fire at the ember stage or the wood-stove stage and save ourselves and others so much grief.

Having a regular meditation practice makes us more aware of what's happening in our mind, the mental undercurrent that tends to go unnoticed when we're caught up in our daily activities and interactions. With meditation, we begin to catch some of the ember-like thoughts and subtle emotions that, left undetected, escalate before we notice them.

Once we've become conscious of the klesha, the next step is to let ourselves feel it—to feel what we're feeling. It sounds very simple, but for many people, this is quite challenging. Some people have difficulty because they've been traumatized. Others have certain emotions that, for whatever reason, they just don't want to face. But, like all the other instructions in the Dharma, feeling what you're feeling is a *practice*. There are ways to train in it, to make gradual progress.

First, start with physical sensations because they're relatively straightforward and provide a good access point. How do you feel physically? When we're out of touch with our body, our kleshas have a greater opportunity to run rampant. On the other hand, when we're present and embodied, it's easier to be in touch with our mind. So notice how your body is feeling—the aches and pains and itches, the sensations of heat and cold, the places where you feel tight or relaxed.

Then look at your state of mind. Is it discursive or settled? What kind of mood are you in? What emotions do you notice? Here it's very important to have an attitude of curiosity and openness rather than judgment. Different things can come up when we allow ourselves to feel what we feel. We may have painful memories or intensely unpleasant emotions. That's to be expected and is no problem. But don't push too hard and make this into an endurance trial. The training should take place, as much as possible, in an atmosphere of acceptance.

To grow in the ability to know what to do when an emotion grabs you, it's helpful to remember three words: embodied, present, and kind. Drop into your body, bring your attention to where you are right now, and be kind. When there's an upsurge of emotion, these three words can help you to deescalate. The main instruction is to stay conscious and, as Tsoknyi Rinpoche has said, "You have to be willing to feel some discomfort." This is, after all, training for both life and for death, both of which are rarely painless.

I've discovered over time that whenever I've allowed myself to feel what I feel, I become more patient with myself and more forgiving. Each time, I find myself able to relax with the feeling a little longer. And here's the thing: while kleshas cause pain, the klesha energy itself is a limitless source of creative power, like an electric current. It's not something you want to get rid of. The trick is to stay present with that energy without acting out or repressing. Doing this—or rather, learning to do this—you might find out something remarkable. In the basic energy of the kleshas, we find wisdom—ungraspable, egoless wisdom—free of grasping and fixation.

In the seventies, when I was being torn apart by kleshas, I was told by almost every spiritual teacher I met to transcend the emotions—to go toward the light. But, fortunately for me, I couldn't figure out how to do it. I couldn't find a way to transcend. I longed to transcend and leave all those tumultuous feelings behind, but I couldn't. Then I received teachings from Trungpa Rinpoche about moving closer to the klesha energy and that changed my life.

12

The First Step to Courage:
Refraining

Here we are, meditators on the path, journeying from birth to death in the bardo of this life. How can we use it to its fullest so that both this life and our death are deeply meaningful? Shechen Gyaltsap, a great spiritual master who died in 1926, put it like this: "Amidst the fleeting clouds of illusion dances the lightning flash of life. Can you say that tomorrow you will not be dead? So practice the Dharma."

To practice the Dharma means not only to meditate and contemplate the teachings but also to apply our understanding in daily life. One of the things that initially drew me to Buddhism was that there were actual methods to help us lead happier, more meaningful lives. There were instructions on what causes our dissatisfaction and pain, and instructions on how to become free of suffering. In fact, this was the aim of the Buddha's teaching.

The true cause of our unhappiness is not outside but inside. Our propensities and negative emotions are what ruin our days, not our supervisor or our nemesis. As is taught again and again, as long as the poisons of the kleshas remain in our mind, we will not find happiness anywhere in the world.

The Buddha taught three main methods for working constructively with our kleshas, which I think of as "three steps to courage." He presented them in order of increasing subtlety and profoundness. The first is refraining from reacting. This is based on the sense that there is something negative about the emotions, so we should do whatever we can to avoid making things worse. With the second method, transforming the kleshas into love and compassion, we adopt a positive view of the emotions: if we use them in the right way, they bring benefit rather than harm. The third method is using the emotions as a direct path of awakening. Here we transcend the duality of good and bad and let the emotions be just as they are.

I've found that the teachings on refraining from reacting can be very unpopular. Once I was giving a talk on this topic and an old friend raised his hand and was clearly upset. He said, "You shouldn't teach this stuff. It's like putting a lid on our feelings. Trungpa Rinpoche would never have taught us this."

Leaving aside that I actually received this teaching from Trungpa Rinpoche, I realized then that it's important to present refraining in a positive light, to present it as an important step toward tapping into the wisdom of emotions, an essential step toward experiencing emotions as a direct path of awakening.

My brother used to tell me, "Whenever you are hungry, angry, lonely, or tired, H-A-L-T." That's an instruction on refraining. Instead of barreling ahead and reverting to old patterns of blaming or judging or otherwise avoiding what we're feeling, we allow space. We halt. We slow down the reactivity.

Often when I teach the practice of refraining, people like my friend ask questions to be sure I'm not encouraging them to hide or to run away from their problems. We're so used to everyone acting and speaking out that if we refrain from doing so, we may feel like we're avoiding things we need to face. But the point of keeping our mouth shut isn't to duck out of heated situations. The point is to give ourselves the time and support to feel what we feel and interrupt the storyline. How we look at things makes all the difference. If we approach refraining as a means of shutting down, it can easily turn into that. But if we approach it as a way of opening up and becoming more allowing of whatever arises, then this practice will serve us well.

In his book *Emotional Rescue*, Dzogchen Ponlop Rinpoche calls this a "mindful gap." It's as if we step back and become more present and awake to what's happening. We allow some space, some mindful space—embodied, present, and kind.

The energy of the kleshas can be very intense. It takes some getting used to. I think of refraining from speaking and acting as becoming familiar with the transformative energy of the emotions. This, I promise, takes patience and time. It's like getting to know an old friend at a deeper level. Our friend's energy challenges us, and yet we stick with them through thick and thin because we love them.

To make it easier to relax with powerful klesha energy, it can be helpful to view it as a process of purifying habitual patterns—of purifying old, unhelpful karma. Since our mind tends to get stuck in repetitive patterns easily, we usually react to new experiences in the same predictable way that we always have. We reinforce old habits by repeating them over and over. But if, on the other hand, we allow a mindful gap, we won't react in the usual way and we can allow the experience simply to pass through us. This weakens our habit. If we do it often enough, we can eventually exhaust the karmic pattern altogether so that it never comes back again.

My experience is that allowing a space before we react predictably is magical. For me, it's what allows for making friends with myself, what allows for clear seeing and a change of direction. Without this mindful gap, without refraining, we just stay stuck in old patterns, wondering, yet again, "How did I get into this mess?"

The practice of halting or refraining is the most basic way of working with our kleshas: don't speak, don't act, get in touch with what we're feeling. It's the first method we need because, when we perpetuate our storylines or act out, we don't have the mental space to apply the other two practices: transforming the emotions and using them as a direct path of awakening. People often want to skip the first stage, but that is doomed to backfire. As Ken McLeod says in *Reflections on Silver River*, "It is often unthinkably frightening to experience what goes on inside you. If you wish to be free, however, you have no choice."

13

The Second Step to Courage: A Positive Take on the Kleshas

*T*he *Seven Points of Mind Training* contains a pithy slogan about the second step to courage, transforming the kleshas into love and compassion: "Three objects, three poisons, three seeds of virtue." "Three objects" refers to three categories—objects that we find pleasant, those that we find unpleasant, and those we have no particular feelings about. The three poisons—craving, aggression, and ignorance—arise in response to these objects. "Three seeds of virtue" suggests that these poisons can be valuable.

Day in and day out, with hardly a break, virtually everyone on this planet experiences the three poisons. Some people are more wrapped up in craving, others in aggression, and others in ignorance, but one way or another we all suffer from the poisons, our reactions to them, and the consequences of those reactions. The kleshas are an inevitable result of the illusion of separateness. Trungpa Rinpoche says in one of his texts:

> From the great cosmic mirror
> Without beginning and without end,
> Human society became manifest.
> At that time, liberation and confusion arose.

From the great cosmic mirror, the basic ground—the open, unbiased ground—we either recognize that we are part of that ground, or we experience ourselves as separate. Once there's that feeling of separation, there's *me* and *you, for me* and *against me, should* and *shouldn't*. And from that, the kleshas emerge. The nature of the kleshas is always the same as the basic ground. But without that recognition, they sure cause a lot of pain.

Since the energy of the kleshas is neither good nor bad, why do we get so captured by them? The answer is because of our thoughts. Only our thoughts make them positive or negative. Because our general propensity is to find the klesha energy hard to handle, we tend to run away from it in harmful ways. This is why we need to slow the process down and allow a mindful gap.

With the practice of transformation, we begin with the mindful gap and then take things a step further. We use our thoughts intentionally to give the kleshas a positive direction. We do this by using the pain of our emotions—that very intensity we usually avoid—to connect with others.

Right now, whatever we are going through, other people are going through the same thing. Whatever is stirring up our heart is stirring up the hearts of countless others. Countless others are feeling disturbed by their emotions, getting caught in their storylines, becoming triggered, and reacting in destructive ways. And this confusion, anxiety, and distress is happening in many ways. It comes in so many flavors. Yet, it is never just *my* pain. Anything I feel is shared by all. When I touch anger, I know the anger of all beings. When I contact the grasping of insatiable wanting, I know the craving of all beings.

All feelings are universal, felt by all of us. We are, in this sense, all in the same boat.

Most of the time when we feel confused, anxious, or distressed, we get wrapped up in our own discomfort, which cuts us off from others. We lose sight of the obvious fact that, just like us, no one likes to feel irritated, depressed, or insecure. No one is indifferent to their own suffering. We know this from experience and from everything we observe. In this essential way, everyone—now and throughout the course of time—is exactly like ourselves. We all want to be free from any form of pain. We all want to enjoy our time on this earth and not experience it as a burden.

The teachings on transformation suggest that we use our emotional pain as a stepping-stone to opening our heart to others. Without experiencing suffering for ourselves, we only have an abstract idea of what others are going through. So when we feel the tug of craving, the burn of anger, the checked-out quality of ignorance, instead of resenting these emotions, we can appreciate them for giving us insight into the experience of others. They can help us develop empathy with all humanity. Thus, the three objects and poisons are transformed into seeds of virtue.

For instance, suppose your most prominent klesha is ignorance. Whenever you're in a tough situation or having a difficult conversation or starting to get overwhelmed, it's as if a plastic sheet goes up between you and the outer world. You can hardly speak or relate. This tendency causes you enormous pain. You feel doomed to go through this awful numbness over and over again. You feel hopelessly stuck.

But here you can try thinking about your numbness

in a different way. Consider that what you're feeling right now is being felt by millions of people throughout the world. None of them welcomes the feeling any more than you do. And beyond the present moment, when you think about the vastness of time, the number of people who've had this unpleasant experience is limitless. Furthermore, this is only one type of suffering. All of us have our own versions, but one way or another we all go through emotional pain throughout our lives. When we tap into what's going on with ourselves and realize the same thing is happening to so many others, there's a real possibility of bringing down barriers between ourselves and others, rather than putting them up. By contemplating our sameness with others, we may begin to question the illusion of separateness.

Having empathy and tenderness for others is based on having empathy and tenderness for ourselves. To the degree that we can feel what we feel, to that degree we will be able to know firsthand what others feel. How can we really know what others are going through and feel tenderness toward them if we haven't felt these things ourselves and developed tenderness for our own sorrows?

Therefore, an important step in transforming kleshas into seeds of virtue is to get in touch with a sense of warm-heartedness toward yourself. Imagine that from this moment on, you were going to accept yourself: your propensities, your shortcomings, the whole package. Imagine if you could trust that you are not a threat to yourself, that you are here to help yourself.

Cultivating a feeling of unconditional warmth to yourself is the foundation of being able to transform your kleshas into love for others. For instance, say you're a compulsive liar. If you simply hate this fact about yourself, you'll always turn away from any opportunity to take a look at what's going on. You'll be too threatened even to ask yourself why you lie so much: what you're trying to achieve and what you're trying to avoid. This denial will give the problem ideal conditions in which to grow, like a mold that thrives in the dark.

But if you develop curiosity and sympathy toward your tendency to lie (not feeding it but exploring it), you'll naturally begin to have empathy for others who do the same thing. You'll understand how much misery this tendency causes—how it prevents people from ever feeling right about themselves, and how that low self-esteem often leads to them striking out at the world. You'll also understand how hard it is to stop lying, even when it becomes painfully obvious how good it would be to stop.

We can only stand in the shoes of others to the degree that we can stand in our own. When we turn a blind eye to our own emotions and propensities, we cut ourselves off from others. It's as simple as that.

14

Two Practices for
Transforming the Heart

There is a practice we can do to develop the courage to feel what we feel. It's called "compassionate abiding." With compassionate abiding as a foundation, we can then practice seeing our sameness with others, just as I've described.

If we have a propensity to feel jealous, for example, we tend to do everything we can to avoid having that unpleasant feeling. But in the practice of compassionate abiding, instead of pushing it away, we open our heart to the feeling of jealousy. Not only do we allow ourselves to feel it, we go as far as to welcome it: we breathe it in generously, as we would breathe in clean country air. Then, as we breathe out, we relax, allow space, and open. Compassionate abiding has the potential to change our whole relationship with jealousy or any other emotion. Instead of being located firmly in the category of "unpleasant" or "poison," the feelings become beneficial. They help us. On the in-breath, we open to the feelings as if opening our arms to a loved one. On the out-breath, we give the feelings limitless space, as if sending them into the vast blue sky.

In addition to breathing in a difficult emotion, we can use it to contemplate our sameness with others. The sharpness of an emotion such as jealousy can remind us how many people have this same propensity. In this very hour, how many people—from every country, every city, every village on the globe—are feeling jealous? How many suffer from envy even more intensely than we do? And of these countless people, how many—unlike ourselves—have little or no perspective on how to work with their painful emotions? Honestly, when I contemplate this, it sometimes makes me cry, and it inspires me not to waste my life just feeling sorry for myself.

Based on this, we can do the practice of *tonglen*, the practice of sending and taking.* In tonglen, we take things even further by breathing in not only our own discomfort but also the discomfort of others. If we're feeling rage, for instance, we can think about how many other people are feeling the same way. In terms of its energetic quality, our own rage is no different from anyone else's. So when we breathe in our own rage, we can imagine that we're also breathing in the rage of people around the world. While doing so, we can think, "May everyone in the world be free of rage. May all beings be free of suffering and its causes." And taking this to its fullest extent, "May all beings awaken to their true nature."

As a natural complement to breathing in emotional pain, when we breathe out we can send others whatever positive emotions and qualities we think would bring them joy and relief, such as love or confidence, health or

---

* If you are unfamiliar with this practice and would like step-by-step instructions, see appendix B.

relaxation. The "sending" part of tonglen is a way of sharing our happiness and good fortune with others, all of whom have the same wish to be happy and fortunate that we do. It counteracts any unconscious habit we may have to keep all the good things to ourselves, to emphasize our own well-being far more than the well-being of others.

Sometimes I ask myself, "What is it really that I'm breathing in?" The emotions are painful, yes, and they cause havoc, but are they really all that solid? If I try to find jealousy or rage, is there anything to grasp? It is taught that both in-breath and out-breath material are empty—just empty form free of all labels, free of good or bad. This absolute way of looking at this practice is well worth pondering.

Through the practice of sending and taking—using the natural alternation of our breath as a medium—we can transform any disturbing emotion into a seed of virtue, a seed of love and compassion. As we gain experience by applying this practice to different feelings and in different situations, we will feel less threatened by our emotional pain. On the contrary, our kleshas will become precious resources for us as they help us arouse the compassionate heart of bodhicitta, the longing to remove the suffering of other beings and to do what it takes to pull that off.

When I asked Trungpa Rinpoche what to do when I die, he said, "Train now in resting in open awareness, and if at the time of death you feel fear or other emotions, do tonglen for all the others who are dying and feeling these same things. Think of relieving them of their suffering and sending them happiness." I've been training like this for many years, especially when I feel fear. I breathe it in and think of others and what they are going through. In this way, I'll open my heart now and at the moment of my death.

15

The Third Step to Courage: Emotions as a Path of Awakening

The third method of working with our emotions—the third step to courage—is to use them as a path of awakening. The idea is to allow ourselves to experience the energy of the kleshas fully and directly. In doing so, we discover that they contain all the wisdom we need to wake up. An unshakable confidence comes from this experience—a confidence that brings fearlessness in life and in death.

As I have said, we all come into this world with co-emergent unawareness, which is a basic misunderstanding about how things are. We believe we have some kind of stable identity, something that makes "me" *me*—something separate from the rest. Based on this misunderstanding, we find ourselves constantly getting hooked by the myriad pleasures and pains the world has to offer. Our mind gets completely wrapped up in kleshas and all the trouble that goes along with them. The teachings say that this painful process will continue until we wake up from our unawareness completely, until we see ourselves and all phenomena as they really are: fleeting, insubstantial, and wide-open with possibility, never separate from the basic ground, never separate from the cosmic mirror.

The term "co-emergent ignorance" is interesting because it implies that ignorance doesn't appear all alone. The Buddha taught that wherever there's confusion, there's also wisdom: "co-emergent wisdom." Whenever we get hooked, whenever our kleshas get triggered, whenever we temporarily lose our bearings and act out in destructive ways, we are in the grip of confusion. But that very confusion is inseparable from our deepest wisdom. In the traditional analogy, confusion and wisdom are like ice and water, which are both made of the same molecules. The only difference is that ice is frozen and water isn't.

Confusion is based on having a frozen view of ourselves and the world. It's a product of our discomfort with the groundless nature of how things are—the cosmic mirror–ness of how things are. Most of us experience that wide-open space as groundlessness. Anger, craving, jealousy, and all the other kleshas are part of this discomfort. If we don't have effective means of working with them, they can ruin our state of mind and harm not only us but the people around us. This is why we learn to work with our emotions.

Using our emotions as a path of awakening is based on simply letting the emotion be, just as it is. I say "simply," but letting anything in our mind simply be is easier said than done. The ego feels at home only when it's meddling, trying to fix things. It's always telling us that we can't leave anything alone. So we need patience and courage if we want to learn how to let our kleshas be.

We first have to give the klesha enough space so we

can actually see what's happening. We need some perspective on our emotion. This doesn't exactly mean distancing ourselves from the klesha; it's more like positioning our mind in order to see clearly. Doing so requires us to practice refraining. It requires a mindful gap before we speak or act. It's hard to have any perspective when we're activated.

Having a clear perspective, we let ourselves experience the emotion as fully as possible. This is similar to letting ourselves feel what we feel, but it goes further. In this practice, we want to learn what the emotion really is. Instead of putting it into a category such as positive or negative, we try to contact its energy directly and intimately, to get to know its very essence. We want to know it, not merely with our conceptual mind, but deeply, with our heart and our full being.

Anam Thubten makes the distinction between ordinary kleshas and conscious kleshas. Ordinary kleshas are what we're familiar with. For instance, when we're in a state of craving, it feels unpleasant, we lack perspective on it, and we usually react in harmful ways. Conscious kleshas are where the wisdom lies. When we go beyond our propensity to be bothered by craving, when we come to experience it as a form of wakeful energy, then the emotion loses its power to disturb us. Instead it becomes something precious, part of the preciousness of life.

By relating to our emotions in this way, we discover their enlightened aspect: the wisdom that is co-emergent with ignorance and confusion. It is always present, in each and every one of our kleshas. To contact it, we allow the klesha just to be what it is. Then the ice will melt and we will experience the open, flowing quality of water.

This isn't easy. Not only does it take practice to contact the wisdom in the kleshas, but it also takes practice to distinguish between the two, between wisdom and nonrecognition. How can we tell whether we're experiencing the neurotic aspect of the energy or the wakeful aspect? Often the clearest evidence is found in our body. Generally, our ordinary kleshas correspond to some form of physical contraction. We feel a tightness in our stomach or jaw, or, perhaps more subtly, in our heart or solar plexus. When our emotions are in the ember stage, this contraction may be hard to detect. But if we practice tuning in to our emotions and our body, then physical tightness can serve as an indicator of when we're caught in ordinary kleshas.

By getting in touch with the physical sensation of our neurosis, we come to know the feeling of wisdom as well. From this point of view, wisdom feels like relaxation, expansion, openness. Instead of fighting with our emotions, we let them be. We don't act them out or repress them. We simply let them be. We simply connect with what they feel like. Instead of tightening up with our strong opinions and storylines, we relax and allow the co-emergent wisdom in our kleshas to speak for itself. If we practice in this way, our emotions themselves will become our most direct path of awakening.

16

Five Flavors of Wisdom

The idea that wisdom and confusion are co-emergent had a profound impact on me the first time I learned about it. It was what first drew me to Tibetan Buddhism and the teachings of Chögyam Trungpa Rinpoche. This was in the early seventies, when I was at the lowest point of my life. I had been to every ashram, visited every guru of every nationality and tradition. I had even tried a weekend of Scientology. But nothing seemed to speak to me about what was actually happening in my life—about the big mess I considered my life to be.

I was living in northern New Mexico, where lots of hippies from Haight-Ashbury had come to explore the many communes and alternative lifestyles. One day, I got into my friend's pickup truck and on the seat was a magazine called *Garuda*, published by Trungpa Rinpoche's students. It was open to an article called "Working with Negativity."

The first paragraph practically knocked me off the seat. Rinpoche said that we experience negativity as "terribly unpleasant, foul-smelling, something we want to get rid of." But, he went on, "if we look into it more deeply, it has a very juicy smell and is very alive." It is "living and precise, connected with reality."

When I look back at that teaching, I wonder how I made heads or tails of it at the time. But I understood the basic message, which was "There's nothing wrong with what you're going through. Just stay with the energy and don't spin off. Then you'll discover something in here that has great value." Not long after that, Trungpa Rinpoche came to New Mexico and I was able to attend his teachings. From that point on, for the next fifteen years or so, I had an ongoing opportunity to go deeper with these teachings under Rinpoche's guidance.

One of the points that Rinpoche often made was that the wisdom we discover in our neurosis comes in different flavors. In the Buddhist teachings, there are five main types of wisdom, which are related to the five primary kleshas: craving, aggression, and ignorance, along with jealousy and pride. Although everyone goes through the whole gamut of emotions, we tend to have one that stands out above the rest. We predominantly experience the neurotic aspect of that emotion, but with the help of these teachings, we can learn to recognize and connect with the wisdom aspect—the awakened, egoless side of the klesha. Then the energy of the emotion can serve to enlighten us rather than bring us down.

Some people, for instance, are frequently caught up in aggression. This klesha comes up in their relationships, at work, in many areas of their life. If they let it go unchecked, it brings great harm to themselves and the people around them. It can turn their life into a living hell.

If we take the approach of using our emotions as the path to awakening, we can look more deeply into the aggression and try to contact its basic energy directly. If we're able to do this without letting our ego get too involved, we'll find a special flavor of the emotion, the flavor of awakened mind. From this point of view, the arising of any klesha becomes a great opportunity to tap into our deepest nature, our open-minded, open-hearted, egoless nature.

In the case of aggression, we find what's known as "mirror-like wisdom." This has the qualities of sharpness and precision; it cuts right through deception and sees everything clearly. Mirror-like wisdom is the particular water that appears when the ice of aggression thaws.

The klesha of craving is co-emergent with "discriminating wisdom." The neurotic manifestation of the energy appears as grasping, needing, wanting. But when we melt this ice by relaxing and letting the energy be, we find its awakened aspect. This is a warm, compassionate quality that goes along with an ability to be connected to the details of life—noticing, taking interest in, having profound insight into the details.

People who are caught up in the neurotic aspect of jealousy tend to be speedy, busy, and critical—wanting to create a neat, uniform world. The awakened aspect is known as "all-accomplishing wisdom." When we experience this energy free from struggle and contraction, it allows us to accomplish things easily for the benefit of everyone involved.

The neurotic aspect of pride is associated with taking up a lot of space. In physical form, this could show up in the way someone who arrives at a meditation retreat sets up their place. In addition to their cushion, they put down fourteen blankets, three thermoses, two shawls, and a pair of slippers. If we connect with the essence of this energy, it becomes the "wisdom of equanimity." Instead of doing so much picking and choosing, there's more of an opening to life as it is—an attitude of letting whatever happens happen, a sense of egolessness.

The klesha of ignorance has the qualities of being dull, lethargic, and out of touch. In its extreme form it becomes numbness. The awakened aspect is called the "dharma-dhatu wisdom." Dharmadhatu roughly means "all-encompassing space." It's the wide-open, fresh, unconditioned space that permeates everything and can accommodate anything.

In the 1980s, I had the opportunity to observe this quality in both its awakened and neurotic aspects in a fellow student. I had known this man only as a teacher. He was a brilliant, spacious, all-accommodating teacher. His words conveyed immense stillness and openness. When he taught, it always resonated with that part in me. In his low-key way, he created an atmosphere of expansiveness.

Over time, I got to know him personally and often experienced him as spaced out, verging on depression—prone to boredom and grumpiness. It was my first experience of seeing the two aspects—the two co-emergent aspects—of one emotional quality manifested so clearly.

The key point to remember is that, in all five of these ways, the wisdom and the neurosis are co-emergent. We can't have one without the other. There's a tendency to think, "I don't want the jealousy; I just want the all-accomplishing wisdom. I don't want any neurotic propensities; I just want the enlightened parts." But that's like a thirsty person in a desert miraculously coming across a block of ice and saying, "I don't care for ice. I'm going to throw it away and look for water somewhere else." There is nowhere else to look. It's just a matter of recognizing that the true nature of ice is no different from thirst-quenching water. In the same way, if we want to discover our own wisdom, there's nowhere to look other than in our own neurosis. We can discover that there's emotion with ego and emotion that is egoless.

When Trungpa Rinpoche started teaching in the West, he began with a completely open field. Because he was among the first people to present Tibetan Buddhism in depth to this part of the world, he had limitless possibilities of how to go about educating people. So I always found it interesting that one of the topics he emphasized early on was the wisdom inherent in the kleshas.

Each of the five wisdom-neurosis pairs is connected to a "buddha family," or "awakened family." Each family is centered on a particular buddha, a fully awakened being who embodies the awakened aspect of the klesha. As Trungpa Rinpoche put it, "You think of enlightenment as one of those serene buddhas: a little smile, so calm, so beautiful to gaze upon. But there are many ways of being sane." On one hand, we can think of wisdom as pure, unbiased, open space, yet it comes in qualities. Enlightenment comes in five basic qualities, five ways of being sane. Becoming familiar with the buddhas is exceedingly helpful not just in this life but, as we will see, in the bardos yet to come.*

Mirror-like wisdom and aggression are connected to the Vajra family. Its symbol, the vajra, is a ritual object that represents indestructibility. The essence of the vajra quality and its mirror-like wisdom is the buddha known as

* A chart outlining the five buddha families and their qualities is available in appendix C on page 190.

Akshobhya. Discriminating wisdom and the neurosis of craving are connected to the Padma family, symbolized by the lotus. Its awakened embodiment is the Buddha Amitabha. Dharmadhatu wisdom and ignorance correspond to the Buddha family and the Buddha Vairochana. The wisdom of equanimity and the klesha of pride go with the Ratna family, symbolized by a jewel, and the Buddha Ratnasambhava. Finally, all-accomplishing wisdom and jealousy are associated with the Karma family and the Buddha Amoghasiddhi. And all these families are connected to their own color, element, season, time of day, and so on—to "any aspect of the phenomenal world," as Rinpoche said.

An essential thing to remember, and one that will serve us well in the bardos, is that the nature of all these buddhas, these awakened beings, is no different from the nature of our own mind. Rinpoche thought it was very important to know what our personal buddha family was because this could serve as a key to contacting our enlightened nature—our buddha nature—which he often referred to as our "basic goodness." Whichever klesha consumes us most frequently and powerfully—whichever one we feel most weary of, most stuck in, most ashamed of—is the most direct gateway to our deepest wisdom, our basic goodness. That is, of course, if we can contact its energy directly without the grasping and rejecting of ego-clinging.

You may accuse yourself of being too angry, too clingy, too spaced out, too envious, or too arrogant, but within each of those disturbing emotions is the personal wisdom of your buddha family—your own style of sanity. You may think to yourself, "I have a terrible anger problem!"

but an enlightened being would turn it around and say, "Lucky you! You have direct contact with the mirror-like wisdom of Buddha Akshobhya. If you don't struggle with that energy, if you become one with that energy, it will wake you up."

Rinpoche wanted us to get to know the quality of our chief neurosis intimately, to become familiar with its "very juicy smell," and to see that as part of the richness of our being. He wanted us to stop wishing we were different, to stop trying to change or hide from our basic quality. Instead he wanted us to welcome it—to let the ice melt into water, simply by being conscious of the klesha, relaxing with the energy, allowing it to just be. But this didn't mean feeding the emotion, or anything like that. Feeding it would be to act it out or to repress it. What he encouraged us to do was rest in the middle of the energy as best we could and let that ability to rest extend gradually and naturally over time.

In his book *Journey without Goal*, Rinpoche says, "Working with the buddha families, we discover that we already have certain qualities. We cannot ignore them or reject them or try to be something else. We have our aggression, our passion, our jealousy, our resentment, our poverty mind, our ignorance, or whatever we have. We belong to certain buddha families already. We should work with them and relate with them and experience them properly. They are the only potential we have, and when we work with them, we see that we can use them as stepping-stones to enlightenment."

At Gampo Abbey, we once had a running joke about who you'd want to be your liaison when you were doing a solo retreat, the person who'd bring things to your cabin. Our system was that the retreatant would leave a note outside the cabin if they needed something, and the liaison would check it and come back with the groceries or whatever it was.

Say you wrote down, "I'd like enough cheese to last me for the week." The joke was, what would a representative from each buddha family bring you? The Vajra liaison would give you seven thinly and beautifully sliced pieces of cheese, separated from one another by wax paper. The Ratna person would send you the whole cheese. Padma would bring the cheese in a basket with a checked cloth adorned by some wildflowers they'd picked. The Karma liaison would fill their time driving to ten stores looking for the perfect kind of cheese, and then complain to you how exhausting that was. The person from the Buddha family would just forget to come. Actually, they'd even forget to check your note.

This joke was related to a game Trungpa Rinpoche invented to help people get a sense of the particular flavor of each buddha family. He called it the "qualities game." I played this with the students at Gampo Abbey a few years ago when I was teaching on the bardos. One person would think of a particular buddha family and the others would try to guess which one it was. They would do this by asking questions like "If this buddha family were a country, what country would it be?" Or "If it were a piece of music, what would it be?"

Once, when I chose Padma, one of the probing questions was "If you were a kind of footwear, what kind would you be?" I (as Padma) replied, "A soft pair of orange slippers." To the question "If you were a profession, what profession would you be?" my reply was "A hospice worker." When people catch on to this game, they can usually guess the buddha family correctly within a few tries. This helps them become more attuned to the specific qualities that go with each family.

We can see the fruition of working with the buddha families in some of the great sages of our time. When I think of my own teachers, although I can't pin them down for sure, I have a sense of their particular quality. His Holiness the Sixteenth Karmapa had a strong Padma family quality. His presence was like golden light, like the sun. He had a warm laugh and would take my hand in the most endearing way.

His Holiness Dilgo Khyentse Rinpoche, a teacher highly revered by all my main teachers, had more of a quality of white light. In his presence, instead of being in the warmth of the sun, it felt more like going out into vast space. His students called him "Mr. Universe." For me, he exemplified the wisdom of the Buddha family.

With Trungpa Rinpoche it was harder to tell. He showed a lot of the qualities, but maybe it was easiest to see his Buddha family quality. He had that spacious, steady, wise presence associated with the dharmadhatu wisdom.

My main living teacher, Dzigar Kongtrul Rinpoche, comes across to many people as strongly Vajra. He's very smart and loves to study the Dharma, and when you hear him teach, he knows how to cut right through. He manifests mirror-like wisdom. But when I got to know Rinpoche better, I discovered that he's also very Ratna. If you visit him, you see that he has all kinds of statues, *thangka* paintings, and other objects. The first time I went to his retreat cabin, I thought, "There's not an inch of space for any more to go in here." But since then, he's fit in quite a bit more. For me, Vajra and Ratna are his basic qualities: his mirror-like wisdom and his wisdom of equanimity.

All of us have our own basic qualities, and for all of us they contain our wisdom. They are the only potential we have. To emphasize that our buddha family qualities are nothing to be ashamed of, Trungpa Rinpoche compared them to ethnic cooking. Whatever culture or part of the world we're from—Africa, South Asia, the Middle East, Europe—we can be proud of the food we cook. It's part of who we are. In the same way, we can be proud of being Vajra or Karma or Padma. It's part of who we are.

The only difference between ourselves and highly advanced practitioners is that we spend most of our time contracting against our emotions and perpetuating neurosis, while they are able to relax with their buddha-family energy, dwell in its wisdom, and display its wonderful qualities. We tend to struggle with who we are, while people such as my teachers step fully and confidently into who they are. They are able to make the best use of their inherent qualities to enjoy life and to benefit others.

17

Experiencing Things As They Are: The Bardo of Dharmata

I've shared with you some of the time-tested instructions I've received for working with emotions. These can be put into practice right now in the bardo of this life or in any of the bardos yet to come. How we work with our thoughts and emotions now is what we'll take with us when we die. We can't put it off until the end; by then it will be too late. So now is the time. How we live is how we die. If we practice these instructions now with a view to how they can help us during the bardos of death, then we'll be well prepared for who knows what.

When we left off talking about the death process, we had reached the stage where the appearances of this life had dissolved. At this point, all the clouds of confusion and habit have dissipated and what remains is only the true nature of our mind: unobstructed, like a pristine, blue sky. In reality, we're never separate from this sky-like nature, never separate from the cosmic mirror. At death, we have a chance to realize this fully and completely.

At the moment of final dissolution, it's as if our awakened nature is handed to us on a silver platter. If we can fully merge with this nature—if we can merge our child luminosity with the mother luminosity—we will attain complete enlightenment right on the spot, "like a son or daughter returning home." However, this opportunity—which practitioners of this tradition consider the greatest in their entire lifetime—goes by in a flash. It is said that the vast majority of people, including most meditators, miss this chance and then go into the next bardo, the bardo of dharmata. *Dharmata* means "the true nature of phenomena," or "suchness," or simply "things just as they are." These names suggest that during this bardo, we directly experience reality without our usual views and opinions, without any conceptual overlay.

I find *The Tibetan Book of the Dead* humorous in a way, because it basically tells us, "If you do what I'm about to tell you, there's no way you won't wake up." Then it tells you what to do and it says, "But if you miss this chance, you'll be in another situation and you can do something else." It keeps going on like this, presenting us with opportunity after opportunity. I like to think of it as the "second chance book." The bardo of dharmata gives us not just one but many second chances.

If we've missed the opportunity to merge with the mother luminosity, then our consciousness finally leaves the body and we go unconscious. Then it's as if we've received a general anesthetic: we enter a completely blank mental state, with no awareness of anything whatsoever.

When we awaken, we're in the bardo of dharmata. Here, compared to our usual experience during the bardo of this life, our heart and mind are much wider open—as open as they can possibly be. This is a state of egolessness. We are temporarily free from our most habitual reference point, our sense of a self. We have a nondual experience. In this way, it's similar to what has already happened after the dissolution of the elements. The major difference is that in the bardo of dharmata, from the basic ground, appearances begin to manifest as powerful sights and sounds, and later as specific forms.

This is, to some degree, how we experience things even now if we slow down enough to notice. In any encounter, first there's open space. Something moves toward me and the encounter is wide-open, full of possibilities, not solidified in any way. I haven't yet formed any concepts about what's happening. Then I perceive just the shape and color of the object. Then it comes into focus, and I'm pretty sure it's a person. Then I might experience aversion, attraction, or indifference. The experience moves from wide-open to more and more concretized and solid.

I think it's worthwhile to try to convey some sense of what it may be like to experience this bardo. Though I obviously can't verify these teachings from my personal experience, they come from a long line of profound and compassionate teachers who have never led me astray. In my experience, the benefits of exploring the more mysterious parts of the Tibetan Buddhist tradition aren't always immediately obvious, but eventually they do become apparent. My overall approach, as I mentioned in the introduction to this book, is to follow the gentle advice of Dzigar Kongtrul Rinpoche: neither rejecting these teachings nor swallowing them whole, but leaning toward them and opening.

The bardo of dharmata is a magnificent display of sight and sound. At first, the projected reality in this bardo comes in the form of brilliant lights filling all of space: vast rainbows and disks and sheets of light. It sounds beautiful, but the colors are so intense and powerful that they can be terrifying. At the same time, there are extremely loud sounds, which Trungpa Rinpoche said are like "the sound of all the musical instruments in the universe being played simultaneously."

Next, according to *The Tibetan Book of the Dead*, these appearances begin to take shape as peaceful and wrathful deities that manifest in a particular sequence. The first five deities are the buddhas of the five families that I've just discussed. Though they are considered "peaceful," they aren't soothing in any familiar way. They have an intensely awake quality. The first one to appear is blue Vairochana, the embodiment of dharmadhatu wisdom, which is the wisdom aspect of the klesha of ignorance. Next is white Akshobhya, who represents mirror-like wisdom, the awakened side of aggression. Then comes yellow Ratnasambhava (wisdom of equanimity, pride), followed by red Amitabha (discriminating wisdom, craving) and green Amoghasiddhi (all-accomplishing wisdom, jealousy).

With the appearance of each of these buddhas, we can attain full awakening by merging with the buddha and its colored light. We do this by relaxing and understanding that we are seeing our own projections. Dzigar Kongtrul Rinpoche said the idea is to gaze right into the light and stay with it. This is easier said than done, for our first instinct is generally to turn away from the light's overwhelming brilliance, which feels disturbing if we're not accustomed to it. At the same time, along with the bright lights, we will see dimmer, more soothing lights, and the tendency will be to be drawn toward those. As it turns out, allowing ourselves to be pulled toward what's habitual and lulling and addictive isn't such a great idea.

In a way, it's silly, but now that I'm familiar with these teachings, whenever I encounter very bright light, light so piercing that I want to turn away, I'm training myself to turn toward it and relax. We are inclined, however, to seek the dimmer and cozier alternatives, even if that means staying stuck in our propensities and all-too-familiar patterns. Trungpa Rinpoche called this being drawn to "comfort mentality," a trait he felt was all too common in his students.

There are two places in *The Tibetan Book of the Dead* where these cozier alternatives are discussed. In both the bardo of dharmata and the next bardo, the bardo of becoming, the seductive dimmer lights lure us back into samsara. These soft lights represent our predictable habitual response to discomfort—we are drawn to what soothes rather than what challenges. In the bardo of dharmata, the dim lights are presented as an alternative to the piercing brilliant lights of wisdom. We have a choice whether to be drawn back into our propensities and kleshas or to stay fully present with the penetrating lights of wisdom. In the bardo of becoming, the dim lights are also presented as pathways to be avoided—pathways to the six realms of samsaric existence. I will describe this fully later in the book.

The best way to prepare ourselves for this situation is to train during this lifetime, as much as possible, in relaxing with the energy of our dominant klesha. Through this process, our own buddha family's awakened quality will gradually reveal itself. Then we will have a better chance of being able to merge with this energy when it appears in its pure, undiluted form during the bardo of dharmata. For instance, if my main klesha is craving, instead of rejecting this craving, I can practice relaxing with its energy and perhaps discover the compassion and warmth of my Padma family wisdom. If I do this often and get very familiar with that wisdom, I may recognize the red light of Amitabha in the bardo and naturally move toward it and relax into it. And if not, not to worry—I'm still making friends with my wide-awake Padma self.

It's important to know that the specific details of what we encounter will be strongly influenced by our cultural orientation and belief systems. A Christian, for instance, might see all the saints. One man told me that since he has no religious beliefs, he might just see a lot of beautiful bunnies. Probably not, but you never know.

Unless we've spent a lot of time studying descriptions of the buddhas and looking at thangka paintings of Buddhist deities, it's unlikely we'll see them just as they're depicted in the teachings. The various Tibetan texts themselves have differences among them. But instead of getting too fixated on details, the main point to remember—the common point in all these teachings—is that we will see wisdom beings in some form that embody the wakefulness inherent in our neuroses. If we've accustomed ourselves to not turning away from or contracting against our klesha energy, we have a chance to realize that this wakeful energy is inseparable from our own true nature—not an external vision that we react to with hope and fear.

According to *The Tibetan Book of the Dead*, the visions of the bardo of dharmata take place over a period of twelve days. In this context, however, a "day" is not the twenty-four-hour period that makes up one human day in the bardo of this life. Most teachers define these days as the length of time one can rest the mind undistractedly in open awareness; in that case, a day could be as short as the time it takes to snap one's fingers.

The appearances during the bardo of dharmata are projections of our mind, but that doesn't make them seem less real than anything we're experiencing right now. Our mind is always projecting. Trungpa Rinpoche wrote that he felt great compassion for beings "who are afraid of external phenomena, which are their own projections." On an everyday level, for instance, we know that our projections about a certain person or group of people can be completely unfounded. We know that many of our biased projections are not believable and that we can think we see a terrifying tiger when it's only a rock.

When we are in the bardo of dharmata, our sky-like mind is temporarily unobstructed by the clouds of habits, biases, and storylines. Our projections no longer have the density and solidity of the objects we encounter in our daily lives. They are more like rainbows. The five buddhas and all the other brilliant appearances are not the product of our usual confused, dualistic mind. They come from our true nature, which is ineffable, unprejudiced, and nondual.

Each of the deities projected in the bardo of dharmata represents a different opportunity for full awakening. The buddha family we resonate with most will give us our best opportunity, but all of these deities are potential doorways. Merging with any of them will be like reuniting with our own wisdom in the form of something seemingly on the outside but inseparable from our own deepest nature. If we train ourselves as much as possible in staying open to the unpredictable, groundless appearances of this life, we may have the instinct to stay open in the bardo of dharmata and become fully awakened.

18

—

Opening to the Sacred World

The Tibetan Book of the Dead belongs to a category of Buddhist teachings known as the Vajrayana, the "diamond vehicle." What makes the Vajrayana different from other approaches in the Dharma is that we take the fruition as the path.

In general, a path goes from one place to another. You step onto a path wherever it begins and you follow it until you reach your final destination. The Vajrayana path to awakening is not like that. The idea is that wherever you are is already the final destination. In other words, you are already enlightened. The job is already done; in fact, it has never not been done. All that remains is for you to recognize and fully acknowledge this fact. You might think this is "mission impossible," but it isn't.

All the Vajrayana methods are based on this view. The Vajrayana path offers countless practices, many of which involve visualization. For instance, you visualize yourself as a buddha at the center of an enlightened mandala. Everyone you meet and all that you see is a deity, a manifestation of enlightened form. Every sound you hear is a sacred mantra, a manifestation of enlightened speech. And everything you think—every movement of your mind—is a display of enlightened mind.

This practice trains us to see everything in our experience as sacred. Through it we discover that we live—and have always lived—in a sacred world. The word "sacred," however, doesn't mean "religious." It means awake already. All that appears is awake already. The word also carries the atmosphere of being precious or blessed—not blessed by anyone, but blessed by its very nature.

Vajrayana practices are profound, subtle, and easy to misconstrue. It's essential to study them under the direct guidance of a qualified and experienced teacher who has no personal agenda other than to help you wake up to your own enlightened nature. However, some familiarity with the basic ideas may help you develop a more positive, optimistic view of death and the bardos, so I think it's worth presenting them in this context.

When we say that our world is sacred and that everyone we meet is a deity, what does this actually mean in terms of our experience? Will we start to see everyone with light streaming out of them like people in religious paintings? Will the traffic noise outside our window turn into a celestial hymn?

On a simple, everyday level, sacred world begins with an attitude of openness and curiosity rather than judgment and dread. When you wake up in the morning, you think, "I wonder what's going to happen today" as opposed to "I've already figured out why today is going to be miserable." Your attitude is "I'm ready for anything," rather than "Oy vey."

We can cultivate this attitude by training in seeing the basic goodness of all that we see, hear, and think. "Basic goodness" isn't about good and bad in the ordinary, dualistic sense. What it means is that everything is the display of wisdom. We can allow everything to be just as it is—without being for or against it, without labeling it as right or wrong, pleasant or unpleasant, ugly or beautiful. This is the attitude of basic goodness. Instead of following our ego's likes and dislikes, we can learn to enjoy phenomena just as they are. Instead of seeing everything through the filter of our habits and propensities, we can appreciate our world just as it is. In describing this, the pioneering Buddhist translator Herbert Guenther said that we begin to experience the world as "imbued with an atmosphere of the miraculous."

When we enter the bardo of dharmata, we've been temporarily stripped of our obscurations and fleetingly encounter the true nature of phenomena. This appears as intensely bright lights and vivid appearances, which develop further into the five buddha families or similar forms for people of different faiths and customs. We encounter basic goodness nakedly and experience the sacred world in all its glory. But unless we've been accustomed to the brilliance and power of this unfiltered world, we'll almost certainly turn away and seek something more familiar and less threatening. We'll miss this chance for complete awakening and go into the next bardo, the bardo of becoming. There we will find appearances that are more familiar.

But before describing the bardo of becoming, let me say more about that crucial moment in the bardo of dharmata when we have the choice to stay or run: to stay with the brilliant projections of our innately enlightened mind, or to go toward what seems more comfortable and familiar. The choice we make then will have everything to do with our way of making choices now.

As human beings, our general tendency is to seek

comfortable situations and, when we find them, to do everything we can to remain there. We habitually want to position ourselves so that we can relax, enjoy ourselves, and not worry. We seek comfort in endless ways: through family, relationships, entertainment, money, food, alcohol, clothing, furniture, sunshine, praise, fame, power, a vacation in Maui, religion, you name it.

There's nothing inherently wrong with wanting to be in our comfort zone. It's healthy to feel safe, relaxed, and pleased by our world. I thoroughly enjoy the sunshine and good food of Maui. I feel I'm truly blessed to occasionally have that experience. If things were always difficult and challenging, we would probably be too stressed and anxious to experience any loving-kindness toward ourselves or to be warm and kind to others. We would have a hard time seeing anything positive about life, to say nothing of experiencing the sacred world. Many people in this world, who might otherwise be inclined to follow a spiritual path, simply lack the minimum comfort, ease, and time necessary to pursue this endeavor. The fact that our lives contain some level of comfort—enough, for instance, to be able to read a book on the bardo teachings—is something to appreciate every day.

The main problem with seeking comfort is that we tend to go too far with it. If we're able to achieve any of the comfort we desire, we tend to turn this pursuit into a full-time occupation. Comfort orientation becomes our way of life; we can become virtually obsessed with avoiding discomfort. We start to think that if somehow we do everything right, we'll be able to stay in our comfort zone forever. This becomes our idea of "the good life."

Then, when comfort eludes us—or when our object

of comfort actually brings us discomfort—we often think it's because we did something wrong. We made a careless mistake, or we didn't have all the information, or we simply blew it. But next time, we think, we can get it right. Next time, we can make all the right moves, like our friends who always look so blissful and fulfilled on their Instagram posts. Odds are, however, that our Instagram friends are doing the same thing we're doing. They're looking at other people and thinking, "If only I could get it all right, just like *them*." They may even have these thoughts when looking at our own Instagram pictures! It turns out that all of us are probably making the same innocent and naïve assumptions about other people.

So we should do a reality check and ask ourselves a simple question: Has anyone in the entire history of the human race been able to achieve permanent comfort? Or, on the other side of the coin, has anyone ever been able to avoid discomfort? Has anyone been able to avoid loss, illness, disappointment, and groundlessness? Has anyone been able to avoid death? As Thinley Norbu Rinpoche used to say, "There is no perfect in this samsara."

We know the answers to all these questions. Challenges and unwelcome events are unavoidable. Groundlessness and death are unavoidable. No period of comfort will last. It's important to enjoy our life, to not be continually overwhelmed by the difficulties of life. It's important to relax and recharge, but when challenges arise, if we always run away, we will find there is nowhere to hide.

Outside the comfort zone is what educators call the "challenge zone" or "learning zone." This is where you get stretched. You want things to go a certain way, but they go a different way. You want to be healthy, but you get sick.

You want to make a good impression, but you make a fool of yourself. You want peace and quiet, but you get noise and chaos. There's no limit to the ways our quest for comfort can be thwarted. But these challenging situations are where all the growth in our life happens.

When we're in our challenge zone, we find out what we're really made of. This is where our propensity to be bothered becomes apparent. It's where all our kleshas and destructive habits come up. It's where our ego flares up, and we tend to push back or freak out. And this is where we have a golden opportunity to start freeing ourselves from our habitual patterns.

Most of the time, we are ruled by our propensities. Our perpetual struggle against life just as it is, is like a thick cloud cover that continually obscures our clear, unbiased mind. But once we've gained some sense of that relaxed, open mind—through formal meditation practice or by experiencing gaps and other moments of spaciousness in our daily life—we can develop an appetite for whatever helps us pierce through the clouds. At that point, we start to have some appreciation for discomfort and disappointment. We may not invite or enjoy these unwanted events and feelings, but we start learning how to make better use of them when they spontaneously arise.

Some people, however, have the tendency to force themselves into difficult situations. This often backfires. If we don't pay enough attention to our body or mind, we can push ourselves past the challenge zone and into the "high risk" or "danger" zone. This is when the discomfort or stress becomes more than we can handle and we don't actually learn anything. Instead, we may end up being traumatized and retreat further into comfort orientation. Of course, sometimes the high-risk zone may be thrust upon us and we have no choice but to make the best of it. But if we are embracing challenge as a tool for growth, we need to be careful not to take things too far.

The Buddha famously advocated a "middle way" approach to spiritual practice and cautioned against going to extremes. One extreme is being obsessed with comfort; the opposite extreme is courting danger. The middle way, in this context, is using whatever naturally comes up as a means of opening your heart and mind. If you practice looking for basic goodness in whatever arises, then you will keep developing, come what may. Gradually you find yourself in a different place. You have new ways of understanding. As time passes, something deepens in you. If you get together with friends you haven't seen in a few years, they may say, "Somehow you've changed." They may notice how you're more open and flexible, how you're less uptight and don't take yourself as seriously as you used to. When you take challenges as opportunities for growth, these changes just naturally unfold. It may be gradual—so gradual we don't even realize it's happening. Nevertheless, we can trust that the unfolding continues moment by moment, day by day.

Life tends to be at its most challenging when we've been half asleep for a long time, dozing in our assumptions of how things are and how they should be. Then some event or insight barges into our dull state of mind and tells us, "Wake up!" Sudden reminders of impermanence can have this effect. The loss of a loved one or a glimpse of our surprisingly aged face in the mirror can jolt us out of our complacency. The truth is not always something we want to hear. But in order to experience our full potential as human beings, we would be wise to appreciate the truth in whatever form it appears.

As we develop an appetite for welcoming the challenges that arise in daily living, our day-to-day experience becomes more relaxed and enjoyable. We become more comfortable with surprise and uncertainty and more able to enter situations that were formerly in the high-risk zone. And when we die, we will be ready for the brilliant and disorienting experiences described in the bardo teachings.

The bright lights of the bardo of dharmata are the lights of raw, uncompromising reality. As I have said, it is tremendously helpful to become familiar with the energy of our dominant buddha family so that when it appears nakedly in this bardo we can merge with it and realize our enlightened nature. But we don't have to think, "I'm Padma, so that means I should be looking out for the red light." Or "I'm Karma, so I'll keep my eye out for Buddha Amoghasiddhi." The bardo of dharmata isn't an academic test that we study for in order to get a good grade. It's more a matter of cultivating a habit of being open to the full scope of life, of going for the stretch instead of the escape route: the reassuring food, the cozy bed, the endless ways we distract ourselves and zone out.

How we live is how we die. If we are willing to spend time in the challenge zone, then how we face the bardo will be similarly courageous, and we will be liberated from all fears. But if we habitually shy away from challenges, then we will be attracted to the path of least resistance. In that case, we will go on to the bardo of becoming, as the vast majority of sentient beings do when they die. But in the bardo of becoming, there is very good news. More opportunities for awakening are yet to come.

19

From Openness
to Concreteness:
An Eternal Pattern

According to the Buddha, all is never lost. This is because every living being—from humans to tiny insects to invisible spirits—has the potential to wake up completely. How wondrous that all beings have that potential!

For anyone who hasn't prepared for death ahead of time, the opportunities for awakening during the bardo of dying and the bardo of dharmata will go by so quickly that they probably won't be recognized. If an insect hits your windshield while you're driving, it will have no awareness of luminosity or deities (unless it's a very special insect) and will immediately find itself in the next bardo, the bardo of becoming. Here its propensities will draw it toward its next birth in one of the realms of samsara.

Our experience of the bardo of becoming is said to be exactly like our experience in a dream. When we dream, we don't go anywhere or do anything with our body. Our body lies asleep in our bed. But we're still able to go through vivid, active experiences that feel real because our mind projects a mental body. This mental body can do all the things our physical body can do. But, because it's less grounded than our waking body, it can do many other wonderful things as well.

In dreams, we can perform miracles: we can fly, we can go through walls, we can find ourselves in spaces and configurations that would be impossible with a solid, physical body. The situation in the bardo of becoming is just like this. Because the mental body is no longer tethered to anything physical, it can do amazing things. But the experience of this bardo is said to be more unsettling than thrilling. It's like being blown about by tremendously powerful winds. After some time in such a vulnerable and agitated state, most beings feel compelled to find a new body.

The experiences of dying, going through the intermediate state, and taking a new birth are said to match closely the daily process of falling asleep, dreaming, and waking up the next day. When we fall asleep—much like at the time of death—our five sense consciousnesses begin to withdraw, one by one: a nightly process of dissolution. At the end of this, we experience a brief gap, which is much like the dawning of the mother luminosity at death. It's a moment of completely open space, of infinite potential. The gap is too fleeting for most of us to notice, but advanced meditators who can maintain awareness while falling asleep can observe and rest in this luminosity.

From out of that open space, the first intimations of form arise. As in the bardo of dharmata, these are egoless projections of our own mind. These appearances are so subtle and fleeting that they're extremely easy to miss. From here, we enter the world of dreams, where what we encounter seems to have more substance. Our mental body continues to have sensory experiences. These experiences don't always make sense according to our everyday logic, but we believe that what's happening is real and we react to it based on our propensities. All this is similar to what happens in the bardo of becoming.

When we wake up in the morning, our normal five senses return and we find ourselves back in a physical body. This is like taking our next birth. Our past experiences—from the night that has ended, from the previous day, and from all our previous nights and days—are gone forever. In many ways, we have a fresh start, a new life.

This pattern of going from openness to concreteness repeats itself in many ways throughout the natural bardo of this life. In fact, it recurs continuously through every single day. Every moment comes to an end. This ending is a kind of death. Something was and no longer is. Before the next event arises, there's a gap, a moment of complete openness and unlimited potential. From out of that pregnant space, a raw energy arises, a subtle intimation of what will next arise. This energy almost instantly solidifies and the next moment of our experience is born.

On a very subtle level, none of our mental or emotional or physical experiences last longer than an instant. It may seem like we're smelling the same lilac scent or feeling the same anger from one moment to the next, but if we slow down enough to notice the continuous, subtle movement of life, it becomes apparent how everything is in a constant state of flux and that there are lots of gaps.

This is something we can verify on the meditation cushion. For instance, we may feel like we're experiencing a solid, uninterrupted siege of anger. But if we look closely, we can see how the anger isn't as monolithic as it appears. Like any klesha, anger ebbs and flows; it manifests in various parts of the body, and there are moments during the experience where our attention goes somewhere else entirely and the anger is no longer felt.

Highly advanced meditators can be aware of all the stages in this process—not only the end of one moment and the beginning of the next but also the energy in between. In the language of Tibetan Buddhism, this three-stage pattern is often described in terms of the "three *kayas.*"

The Sanskrit word *kaya* literally means "body," but here we are talking about different levels of reality, from most subtle to most coarse. *Dharmakaya* refers to the basic space from which all form arises. *Sambhogakaya* is the energetic aspect, the subtle form behind the solidified manifestations that make up our day-to-day experience. *Nirmanakaya* refers to the concrete phenomena that we can perceive with our ordinary faculties.

From one point of view, the three kayas are stages that keep repeating themselves from moment to moment. But we can also say that all three are present at all times. In the open space pregnant with possibility, there's always an energetic potential. And these two aspects of reality—space and energy—always manifest in concrete forms.

On a larger scale, we can connect the three kayas to the three main opportunities for awakening in the bardos. At the moment of death, the chance to merge with the open, empty mother luminosity is a chance to merge with the dharmakaya aspect of our own nature. In the bardo of dharmata, there's the possibility of merging with the bright lights and peaceful and wrathful deities. These energetic appearances are manifestations of the sambhoga-kaya aspect of our own nature.

Finally, in the bardo of becoming, we encounter the dreamlike appearances of the nirmanakaya aspect of our nature. At this stage, there is no longer a chance for immediate enlightenment, but we can go to what's called a pure realm. Or, if we've prepared well during this life, we can have some control over where and in what form we take our next birth.

20

—

Entering the
Bardo of Becoming

*T*he *Tibetan Book of the Dead* tells us that if we miss our brief chance to awaken during the bardo of dharmata, we will then go unconscious and wake up in the bardo of becoming, which is said to last at the most forty-nine days. The word "becoming" refers to the idea that at this point in our journey we can become anything. We can be reborn as any type of living being and in any place where beings exist. This intermediate state is also known as the "karmic bardo of becoming" because we are pulled strongly by our karma. In other words, our direction is determined by all that we have done, said, and thought—and the imprints these actions have left on our mind.

Again, this is the Tibetan worldview, which you may or may not subscribe to. But even in terms of this life, we can see how we continually create our future reality through the actions of our body, speech, and mind. Every time we get carried away by our kleshas, say by lashing out at someone or putting ourselves down, we reinforce our self-destructive habits and intensify our struggle against life as it is.

This conflict tends to be reflected in our external environment. If we let our harmful tendencies get the better of us, our world tends to become increasingly unfavorable and sometimes even hostile. On the other hand, if we work day by day—to the best of our current ability— on connecting with our heart and opening our mind, our outer situations and the people we encounter will become more friendly and hospitable. In this way, whether we are in the middle of this life or in a gap between lives, we are always pulled by karma. We are always "becoming." As Trungpa Rinpoche would say, "The future is open."

According to the traditional teachings, when we enter the bardo of becoming, we go through experiences with our mental body that feel every bit as real as when we're dreaming. In the bardo of dharmata, we experience, however fleetingly, the true nature of reality without the filter of ego. But in the bardo of becoming, all our habitual patterns return. Even though our entire world has changed, we've come back to the familiar sense of self, the feeling of "I'm *me*, this individual being that is distinct from everything else." In a way, this makes things feel more familiar. We're in a world that makes sense to us, and chances are we have no idea that we've died.

Just as in your dreams, you can go beyond the limits of your physical body. Even if you died at an old age and had terrible hearing and eyesight, you now have all your sense faculties working properly. Even if you were stiff and weak at the end of your life, your mental body is now light and agile.

In this bardo, your awareness is said to be seven times clearer than before you died. You can read the minds of people who are alive and hear what they're thinking about you, which may cause deep distress. For instance, your loved ones may become obsessed with your money and quarrel with each other, saying unflattering things about your stinginess. They may fight over who gets what and be contemptuous of your prized possessions. They may take something you cherished and toss it into the dump.

For this reason, we're encouraged to give away possessions before we die and to state our wishes clearly in a will. When we die, the less there is that bothers us, the better. The more we let go of our preferences and our attachments to things now, the better.

A close friend of mine wrote out a precise list of who should get each of her things after she died. However, she'd unintentionally told two different people they could have her pearl necklace. The bad feelings this provoked were hard to witness. I imagined my friend looking down from the bardo of becoming, distraught about how her carefully laid plans had gone astray!

Another friend was very attached to her possessions and tried to give them all away before she died, but found she couldn't let them go. After her death, the volume of her belongings was so overwhelming that her friends just couldn't handle it. So they built a huge bonfire and threw in boxes and boxes of stuff. There were years and years of carefully labeled photographs that now meant nothing to anybody, and into the fire they went. The moral of the story is to "let go of all attachments to this life" while you still can. That way, there will be far less to upset you in the bardo.

I've expressed in writing my wish for silence when I'm dying. But it occurred to me recently that if I'm too attached to this wish, it's a recipe for disappointment. The last thing I want to do at death is to be bent out of shape because there's too much noise!

It's said that in the bardo of becoming the first thing you do is go back to where you lived. You see your family. They're weeping and you don't know why. It's confusing. You try to communicate with them, but they don't reply. Then it dawns on you that they don't even know you're there. *The Tibetan Book of the Dead* says the pain you feel is as intense as "the pain of a fish rolling in hot sand." This is why the teachings suggest that when someone we know has just passed away, we should keep reminding them that they've died. Doing so will lighten their confusion and help them accept what's going on. We could remind them when we're beside their body, or even later and at a distance. Unless someone tells them they're dead, they may go on for a long time without realizing it.

Life in the bardo of becoming is said to be extremely unstable. If you think about a place, you can appear there instantaneously. You could think about Brooklyn and then immediately find yourself walking down the street in Brooklyn. The next moment you could think of Kenya and be in a house in Kenya. Sometimes these experiences are pleasant and sometimes they're not, but the overall feeling is disorienting and exhausting. You never get a chance to rest. As time goes on, you crave a physical body more and more.

They say this bardo is very dim, which for me is an uncomfortable thought. You can see other bardo beings who have died around the same time, but you can only communicate with them briefly because everyone is always on the move. If you have the habitual pattern of running away from whatever bothers you, then in this bardo you'll be constantly on the run. This is not part of the tradition, but sometimes I have conversations with friends who have died. I do this during the forty-nine days after their death, hoping to help them make a smooth transition. The main advice I give them is "Don't run. Slow down. Don't make any quick moves. Face whatever scares you." That's good advice for life as well.

Some of you will remember the story from my book *When Things Fall Apart* about my childhood friend Suzy and her recurring nightmare. When we were about ten years old, she dreamed every night that she was being chased by monsters. One day, I asked her what the monsters looked like and she didn't know because she was too terrified and always running. This apparently got her curious and the next night she got up all her courage and turned around. Trembling all over, she did the unthinkable. She looked at them. At first, they rushed toward her, and then they just melted away. And that was the end of her nightmares. This is a story to remember in the bardo of becoming.

In this bardo, the atmosphere often feels threatening because the various elements tend to appear as enemies. For instance, when the air element feels like an enemy, there are hurricanes and tornadoes. When the earth element feels hostile, you experience earthquakes and landslides. The water element can bring forth tsunamis and floods. This brings us back to a repeating theme: how we relate to frightening events now will be how we'll relate to them in the bardo of becoming. The important part to contemplate is this: Do we get all worked up and lose our willingness to care for others, or are we more inclined to stay present, right there with our feelings, and with concern about what others are experiencing?

Some books on the bardos speak of a life review and a judgment that take place, as is described in many of the world's religions. You see everything you've done in your life—every action, right or wrong, important or unimportant, flattering or unflattering. The judge is no one other than your own conscience. In this state, you can clearly see your actions and the motivations behind them, and this can be very painful. For monastics, we look at our lives every new moon and full moon day in what is called the *sojong* ceremony. The idea of this ceremony is to acknowledge, as completely and compassionately as we can, all the actions we regret from the last few weeks and throughout our whole life. Then, after death, there will be nothing to be ashamed of, nothing that hasn't been faced and let go, nothing that holds us back.

One of the points most emphasized in the bardo teachings is the power of positive and negative thoughts. Because our awareness is so much sharper than usual, one positive thought could interrupt the momentum of a painful or scary experience and immediately bring you somewhere much more pleasant. But the reverse is also true: one negative thought can suddenly bring you down into the depths of suffering. This is, of course, as crucially important right now as it is in the bardo of becoming.

For this reason, in my conversations with friends in the bardo, I always encourage them to think positively. Instead of complaining and feeling resentment—such as about how they're burning up all your beloved photos—I encourage them to think of people and places they love and things that inspire them, and I encourage them to open their hearts to others.

Whether or not we believe that such an intermediate state really exists, we can still apply and benefit from these teachings while we're alive. Though our thoughts right now aren't quite as powerful as they're said to be in the bardo of becoming, their tremendous power to carry us away should never be underestimated.

Our ability to interrupt the momentum of negative thought patterns can be greatly enhanced through meditation practice. I've learned this to be true from my own experience and from talking to many students about meditation over the years. The more we practice, the more we can get used to being present with thoughts, emotions, and circumstances that used to sweep us away. Instead of continuing to react solely based on habit, we can gradually develop some appropriate distance from the compelling events taking place in our mind and in our perceptions. We can get better at catching our emotions at an earlier stage, before the storylines fully kick in and turn our little sparks and embers into destructive blazes.

To prepare for the groundlessness of the bardo of becoming, the best thing we can do now is to work on dealing with the groundlessness of this life. This will pay off during our lifetime, no matter what we believe happens after death. If we come to terms with the unpredictable, transitory quality of our mind's experiences, we will be less subject to being blown around like a feather in any chaotic situation we encounter. If we become deeply familiar with our own mind's qualities and potential—how surprising our mind is, how malleable, how workable—then we will have more freedom of choice, whatever happens. Even if our mind becomes tremendously speedy and unstable, as is said to happen in the bardo of becoming, we may have some ability to direct it in a favorable way.

In any intense or difficult situation we have in life, it helps to be as open and present as possible. This will always benefit ourselves and those around us more than panicking and running away. The same is true for the bardo of becoming, when our own capacity to stay present is the only stability we'll have. Again, this capacity depends on whether we have cultivated it before we die.

A long time ago, I remember hearing a story about two Buddhist monks who lived at a temple in California. They set off to prostrate the whole length of the West coast, from the top of Washington to the bottom of California. They'd take three or four steps and then go down on their knees and touch their hands and forehead to the ground. Then they'd stand up, take a few more steps, prostrate again, and so on—for hundreds and hundreds of miles.

The monks' intention was to relate with whatever occurred during the trip as a projection of their own mind and to always try to see their interconnectedness with all they encountered. This was the open and courageous attitude that they aspired to hold. Whatever happened was not separate from them. There was no division between the monks and their environment. From their studies and practices, they understood—at least conceptually—that whatever arose was not separate from their mind.

The monks went on a journey to cultivate fearlessness—as well as love and compassion and a deep sense of our interconnectedness. Their journey was also a superb training for the journey through the bardo.

By prostrating, the monks were honoring not only

the Buddha, but their entire experience—whatever and whomever they saw, including themselves. They probably saw more blacktop and pebbles than anything else, but it didn't matter: they considered everything worthy of prostration.

Eventually, their journey took them through a neighborhood in Los Angeles. A group of young people saw these bald men in robes behaving very strangely, and they surrounded them. They started taunting them and laughing at them and trying to intimidate them. One young man picked up a sharp piece of metal. He started swinging it around right in front of them threateningly, as if it were a weapon.

One of the monks became so afraid that his knees were literally knocking together and he could hardly stand up. He had no idea what to do. Then he remembered the purpose of their journey and the view of interconnectedness. So he prostrated to the young man with the weapon, seeing him as not separate from himself.

At that point, the whole thing just stopped. The young man with the weapon was so floored at being prostrated to that he and his friends moved aside and let the monks go on. The monks probably prostrated much faster until they got away, but I thought this was an amazing story about how differently the world responds when we embrace rather than reject it. If we can develop this attitude and bring it with us into bardos and other difficult situations, we will be doing ourselves a great favor.

Once we reach the bardo of becoming, the texts stop talking about immediate opportunities for full awakening, but the tradition says that at this point, there's still a wonderful thing that can happen. We can be reborn in a pure realm. This may sound like the Christian idea of heaven or even something dreamt up by Walt Disney, but according to Trungpa Rinpoche, a pure realm is a place where you and everyone else have almost no kleshas and your minds naturally turn toward awakening. There are many pure realms, more than I am even familiar with, which suit beings with various temperaments and karmic connections. Each of these realms has its own particular atmosphere, but each is conducive to developing wisdom and compassion.

Sometimes Tibetan people like to discuss which pure realm they would like to be born in. I heard that Dilgo Khyentse Rinpoche and his wife Khandro Lhamo would get into playful arguments about this topic. His wife said she wanted to be born in Sukhavati, the pure realm of the Buddha Amitabha. Rinpoche wanted to go to Guru Rinpoche's Copper-Colored Mountain and he tried to convince her to aspire to be born there as well. His closest disciple was his young grandson, Rabjam Rinpoche, who would sometimes witness these debates and side with his grandmother. He also wanted to be born in Sukhavati.

But one night, Rabjam Rinpoche dreamt that he was in an airplane with his grandfather. Khyentse Rinpoche said, "Look!" and below them was this beautiful, angelic place. He said, "This is Sukhavati. It's where you get out." The boy said, "But where are you going?" Khyentse Rinpoche pointed into the distance to a place where there was thunder and lightning and earthquakes and all hell breaking loose. He said, "I'm going there, to the Copper-Colored Mountain." And then his grandson said, "I want to go where you go. I'm going with you."

In the Mahayana tradition of Buddhism, we take

what's known as the "bodhisattva vow." This is a promise to work wholeheartedly on our spiritual path so that we can fully awaken and be of maximum benefit to others. Once we attain enlightenment, instead of going off and enjoying our awakened mind in private, the idea is to keep coming back to the world, over and over again, to help others become liberated from suffering. We vow to do this until samsara is completely empty. We take on this seemingly impossible task willingly, even joyfully. And why, you might ask, would anyone do such a thing? The answer to this has slowly dawned on me over many years of supposedly keeping this vow: when compassion and love are unconditional, the only thing that makes sense is to save everyone on the boat with no one left behind.

In this context, to be reborn in a pure realm may sound like it goes against the bodhisattva vow. But the point of going to a pure realm is actually to speed up our spiritual journey so that we're in much better shape to benefit others. Maybe going to a pure realm is similar to going on retreat. In both situations the atmospheric conditions are conducive to rapid progress toward awakening. But when you go into a retreat, you don't have the idea of staying forever. You intend to return to your life and use what you've learned for your own sake and for the sake of others. If you aim to go to a pure realm, this is your intention as well.

The way to be reborn in a pure realm—or to make any choice in the bardo of becoming—is to direct our thoughts where we want to go, and call out for support if necessary. This is not to be understood as thinking that someone will come to your rescue. The idea is more that you ask for the courage to stay present and to keep your mind and heart open and not get caught in old habitual patterns. In his commentary to *The Tibetan Book of the Dead*, Trungpa Rinpoche says that calling out for support in the bardo "is not a request to an external deity," but rather a method of directing the mind, of arousing the mind's inherent desire for good. This is a positive way of harnessing the increased power of our awareness. But if we've never aspired during this lifetime to be reborn in a pure realm, we're not likely to do so for the first time in the dreamlike bardo of becoming. This is why Buddhists of many traditions make daily aspirations to be reborn in a pure realm, where they have the best chance to get better at benefiting others.

This is yet another example of "how we live is how we die." It's not only our neurotic propensities that go with us from life to life. All the positive habits we've cultivated will also remain in our mindstream for as long as we keep reinforcing them. Then they will be there to support us even when we find ourselves in a situation, such as the bardo of becoming, where almost everything feels disorienting.

Since we never know when we'll die or what will happen next, it's valuable to cultivate positive thought patterns intentionally so they'll kick in when we need them most. When Mahatma Gandhi was assassinated, his words immediately after being shot were "Hey Ram, Hey Ram," a Hindu invocation of God. It's unlikely that these words would have come to him without prior training in calling on Ram during unexpected and distressing events. In a similar way, we can train in automatically having positive thoughts whenever shocking or disappointing things happen out of the blue. This could be any event, big or small—whether we slip on a banana peel, we spill ink on our new white shirt, or the doctor tells us we don't have long to live.

Trungpa Rinpoche joked that if you always say "Oh, sh-t!" whenever something shocking happens, "Oh, sh-t!" could end up being the last thought you have in this life. When we come to know our mind more precisely through meditation, we see the power of every thought to create a ripple effect that can strongly influence our whole experience. Unless we're in a clear state of mind where we can recognize the insubstantial nature of our thoughts, each thought will lead to something else: another thought, an emotion, an action, further thoughts, and so on. So if we believe that consciousness continues after death, our last thought in this life is extremely important. It has the power to send us off in a certain direction, and its effects will keep rippling through the bardos.

For this reason, Trungpa Rinpoche recommended gently shifting our habitual reaction of shock to something more open, such as "Wow!" or "A la la!" It would be much better to start our bardo experience with a feeling of amazement rather than one of rejection or panic. Even if "Sh-t" is already out of your mouth, you can still keep going and say, "Wow!" This will help you train your mind in a better habit and give you a good laugh at the same time.

During these kinds of moments, I've been training myself to say OM MANI PADME HUM. This mantra, known as the "Mani," invokes the bodhisattva who embodies compassion: Avalokiteshvara in the Tibetan tradition, or Kwan Yin in the Chinese. Saying the Mani is a way of surrounding your situation and whomever you're thinking about with compassion and love. Some Tibetans carve this mantra onto stones or say it millions of times throughout their lives in order to imprint compassion in their hearts and minds so that it's always available. It becomes like the air they breathe. One time when I was in retreat, I met a bear in the woods at dusk. That definitely stopped my mind. I stared at the bear and the bear stared at me and then I took off running, yelling OM MANI PADME HUM at the top of my lungs.

If we work on developing compassion in this life, that will also serve us enormously in the bardo of becoming. We will realize that countless others are in the same boat and we will understand how much pain they are going through. We will be less self-concerned and therefore feel less threatened.

Our compassionate heart can also help us see through the dreamlike quality of the bardo of becoming. It can help us wake up within the dream. For instance, if the water element is rising up as an enemy and a tidal wave is coming at you, your compassion might make you look around to see if there's someone else you could save. Right away, you won't be as caught in the whole illusion because you won't be so focused on yourself—this seemingly real, unchanging "me."

In the *Jataka Tales*, the traditional collection of stories about the Buddha's former lives, there's a story that illustrates the power of a single compassionate thought. The future Buddha and another man were suffering in a hellish existence and were being forced to push a huge boulder up a steep mountain. The guards would whip them until they got to the top and then the boulder would roll down and crush them. Then they would have to start over again—and again and again. During the whole experience, the future Buddha was consumed with anger about what was happening to him, but one day he had a thought that interrupted the momentum of his rage. He realized how much his partner was also suffering and told the man to rest while he tried to push the rock by himself. Of course, this provoked the guards, who beat the future Buddha even harder, but his one compassionate thought had popped him out of his hellish mentality, and from then on he was always born in situations where he could wake up further and further.

Our felt sense of existing as a separate, special self is at the root of all our torments in life and in death. The more we can let go of our fixation on this illusory "me" during this life, the more we'll be free of that fixation in the bardo of becoming. The more we can realize the dreamlike nature of our life right now, the better chance we'll have of realizing that the bardo of becoming is also just like a dream. And when we realize we're in a dream, we may have some say about where that dream is taking us. Then we can use the clarity of our bardo mind to make a smart choice and go toward a pure realm or a favorable rebirth where we can benefit others.

21

Heart Advice

Never underestimate the power of warmth—right at this very moment, and when we die. In particular, there are two kinds of warmth that soften us up and make us more decent, loving beings. One is the warmth of kindness and extending ourselves to others, thinking of them rather than remaining completely self-centered. The other is the warmth of devotion: love for one's teachers, those who have shown us the truth. Both come from the warmth of the heart. Both make our lives deeply meaningful. Both bring down the barriers between ourselves and others.

The warmth of kindness to others is easy to understand and generally not controversial. We may feel caught up in our own ego trips, but still we want closeness with others. We want to bring down those barriers and feel an outflow of tenderness and caring. We aspire to awaken the compassionate heart of bodhichitta and have it flourish.

Fortunately, for all of us, certain teachings and practices can help us do just this. A practice like tonglen, for instance, supports the flourishing of bodhichitta.* For centuries, ordinary, confused people like you and me have

---

* For more bodhichitta practices, see *The Places That Scare You.*

been drawn to these teachings and practices and have devoted time and effort to making them an organic part of their actions, words, and thoughts. With their actions, they manifest caring and concern. With their speech, they manifest nonaggression and open-heartedness. Even their minds gravitate more naturally toward thinking of others' benefit. They've uncovered qualities that have always been there, qualities that are our birthright.

This description, of course, presents the ideal. But all of us can move in this direction as our genuine concern for the welfare of other beings grows. A surprising number of people are training exactly like this—falling down frequently, learning from their mistakes, and continuing forward, step by step, inch by inch, to uncover the warmth of bodhichitta.

To the degree that our heart has opened in life, to that degree it will open at death. In this way, when we move through the bardo of dying and beyond, we will automatically think of others. Instead of our heart contracting in the bardo, it will expand. We may get captured by fear and start to withdraw into ourselves, but then, because of our former practice, we'll naturally pull ourselves out of a tailspin. We'll look around to see who is there with us, and we'll wonder what they are going through.

Since a positive state of mind is so important at death and in the bardos, this openheartedness toward others will make for a peaceful and positive journey. It will provide the perfect causes and conditions for awakening at any point during the in-between stage between death and birth.

Unlike the warmth of kindness, the warmth of devotion to a teacher can be surprisingly difficult for many of us even to consider, let alone embrace. For some, the mere word "devotion" can be unsettling, particularly when connected with spiritual teachers. This is because, in modern times, too many teachers have actually harmed their students and betrayed their trust. And yet, believe me, devotion to an authentic teacher, who only cares for your benefit, is magical. To quote Dzogchen Ponlop Rinpoche, it is "a key that unlocks the doorway to the most profound experiences of mind."*

Sometimes we are fortunate enough to meet people who appear to live fully in nowness, people who resonate deeply with the openness of our own being. I have met enough of these people to know that even thinking of them connects me with open awareness, with the awakened nature available to all, yet recognized by relatively few.

This recognition of our nature is precious and miraculous. As I've often heard, what we seek is already ours. Ultimately, there is only one teacher: mind's true nature. When I connect with this, it feels like I'm connecting with my deepest potential. This is why I feel boundless gratitude to all the teachers who have introduced me to the nature of mind and to the sacredness of the world and its beings. Real devotion, it seems to me, is openhearted receptivity to things just as they are.

When I met the bear in the woods and began chanting OM MANI PADME HUM, I wasn't calling on an external deity to save me, but rather making a connection with the compassionate blessings that are always available to that

---

* For a more thorough discussion of this topic, see *Welcoming the Unwelcome*, chapter 19: "Learning from Our Teachers."

bear and to me. So whether it's today or when I've died, I know that calling to my teachers, or to wisdom figures like Kwan Yin or Avalokiteshvara, is really opening myself to a source of blessings inseparable from my own basic nature. It's opening to that part of my nature beyond propensities or kleshas—or any style of self-centeredness.

This is, without a doubt, a heartfelt, sublimely connected experience. For me it's an experience of devotion. This devotion is not mindless adoration or idealization of a specific person. Yet it's connected with remembering specific teachers and what they've shown me. When I walked the plank in that virtual reality experiment, it was devotion that enabled me to "jump." After an extended period of terror, I thought of Trungpa Rinpoche and heard his unmistakable, high-pitched voice say, "You can do it." That's all it took to connect me with my innate courage.

Now and in the bardo, I know that warmth is the key. Thinking of the welfare of others and opening my heart to the blessings of my teachers—I put my trust in these two wondrous methods.

22

The Six Realms

Once we enter the bardo of becoming, unless we go to a pure realm, we're on track to take another birth in samsara, the seemingly endless cycle of birth and death. Just as in the bardo of dharmata, cozy, soft, seductive lights of different colors will appear. Unless we have developed the strength and courage to avoid their lure, these lights will draw us back into one of the realms of samsaric existence.

We've been trapped in samsara for longer than we can remember—longer than anyone can remember. In the classic metaphor, a living being in samsara is like a bee trapped in a jar. The bee buzzes up and down, going from the top of the jar to the bottom and back again, but it can never get out and fly in the open air. Similarly, in samsara, we go up and down—from happy lives to miserable lives and back again—but we remain trapped in this cycle. And even though there are some pretty good births in samsara, overall this cycle contains a great deal more dissatisfaction than joy.

In the traditional teachings, samsara is divided into six realms. These are usually listed in order from most painful to most pleasant: the hell realm, the hungry ghost realm, the animal realm, the human realm, the jealous god realm, and the god realm. They are six categories of experience of life within the jar. But the Buddha, in his very first teachings, explained that there is a way out of samsara altogether. Eventually all of us can and will become liberated from the realms and enjoy the open air of awakening. As I once heard Dzigar Kongtrul Rinpoche say, "Sooner or later, it's guaranteed."*

The traditional teachings speak about these realms as if they are literal places, as real as the familiar environment we currently find ourselves in. Trungpa Rinpoche, however, presented the realms as psychological states. He understood that many people in the West were turned off by any talk of the afterlife, especially if they had been threatened during their upbringing with various kinds of hell. I myself was not very open to contemplating the realms until I heard Trungpa Rinpoche's teachings. Instead of talking about them as actual physical locations that we could find on some sort of cosmic map, he taught the realms as projections of our own reactive emotions. The phrase he used to describe them was "styles of imprisonment."

The idea is that when you're in the grip of a powerful emotion, that klesha is running you and your world. It determines your state of mind and the whole way the environment appears to you. You feel trapped in an entire realm created by the klesha. We experience this in our day-to-day lives. Again and again, we find ourselves in a habitual place of painful emotion. We don't know how we got there, and we don't know how to get out. But it feels very familiar.

* An illustration of the six realms of samsara is available in appendix C on page 192.

Hell is the realm of anger and aggression. The traditional teachings refer to many types of hell, but most of the hells fall into two categories: hot and cold. In the hot hells, the basic idea is that everything is on fire and you can't get away from the burning. In the cold hells, everything is ice. You're naked and freezing and your skin erupts in all kinds of ghastly cracks. Whichever version of hell you're in, one of the main characteristics is that it seems to last forever.

For some people, an enraged mind feels like fire; for others it's more like ice. Either way, you feel trapped by its intensity. In the grip of anger, the only escape seems to be through acting out. But instead of bringing relief, your aggression only prolongs and amplifies the torment, making the heat hotter or the cold colder. You feel claustrophobic and desperate. This is why the torment of anger can seem to last an eternity; it feels like a trap from which there is no way out. It's said that in the hells, there are compassionate beings who try to help you. In the hot hells, they offer you water; in the cold hells they offer fire for warmth. But you are so convinced that everyone is against you that you refuse their help.

It's easy to see how this applies even in the relative comfort of our ordinary human world. My dear friend Jarvis Masters has been in prison for more years than he was out. In that time, he's witnessed many people in hell. In prison, the suffering from aggression and despair is immense. What he tries to do, along with extending friendship, is to convince his brothers not to escalate their pain by attacking other inmates or the guards. He tries to show them how not retaliating will bring better results and lessen their pain. He says that some people do listen to him and think that what he's saying makes sense, but very few can break their old habit of wanting revenge. Very few can refrain from entertaining these thoughts and acting upon them.

In the hungry ghost realm, the beings have grotesque descriptions. Some of them have an enormous empty belly, but their mouth is about the size of a dot and their throat is as thin as a hair. They're always hungry and can never take in nearly enough food to satisfy them. Traditionally, the emotion this relates to is greed, but Trungpa Rinpoche's term was "poverty mentality." This is a feeling of neediness that can never be satisfied. No one ever loves you enough, there's never enough of anything, you're always left out. You constantly feel you're starving. Everything that happens makes you feel deficient, like a loser.

The animal realm is associated with the klesha of ignorance. But the word "ignorance" can be misleading, because one might mistake it for stupidity. In their own way, animals are very intelligent. I often think of the time I spent a week trying to outsmart a squirrel that was eating all the seeds in my bird feeder. I tried everything I could think of. I found places to hang the feeder that I thought were impossible for the squirrel to get to. But the squirrel always outsmarted me.

Though animals tend to be highly intelligent in their own sphere, for the most part they don't have flexible minds. The squirrel may be a genius in terms of stealing seeds, but it would have no idea how to go about surviving in an unfamiliar environment. When things get unpredictable, when their routine gets interrupted, beings in the animal realm become bewildered and helpless.

"Animal realm" doesn't necessarily mean being an animal per se. Rather, it has to do with a certain mentality that is very familiar to many human beings. Instead of "ignorance," I prefer to think of it as "ignoring." When you're outside of the sphere where you function well, you feel anxious and resent being challenged. But instead of going into an emotion like rage, you deal with your anxiety by ignoring. You pretend it's not happening. You block out the situation by surfing the internet or playing solitaire or doing something mindless. The statement that encapsulates this mentality is "I'm just trying to get by." You're only willing to operate within your sphere of confidence and you don't want to be bothered with anything more. It's a kind of status quo mentality.

The hell, hungry ghost, and animal realms are called the "lower realms" because the suffering there is the most intense. This is obvious in the descriptions of the hell and hungry ghost realms, but maybe less so for a lot of the animals we observe. Cherished pets, for example, appear to have pleasant, comfortable lives. But in general, animals spend much of their time being afraid. They don't really know what threats are out there or who might be eyeing them as a meal, so they live in a state of constant fear. You can see this in every kind of animal: on land, in the air, and under the sea. Those sweet little chickadees who eat from your hand don't just take the food. They look around nervously to make sure nothing is going to get them.

The human realm is more favorable than the lower realms because the suffering is not relentless. Pain alternates with pleasure. In the hungry ghost realm, we want, want, and want, but we never get. In the human realm, we also want much of the time—but sometimes we do get. We succeed just often enough that it seems like we could figure out a way to get what we want all the time. This sets up the predominant mentality of the human realm: we hope to have only pleasure and no pain. We have this constant, naïve wish that we could somehow stop the alternation.

We spend our time trying to be with people we like and avoiding people we don't like; trying to be in comfortable, pleasant situations and avoiding uncomfortable, unpleasant ones; trying to hold on to whatever pleasure we have and trying to keep all pain at bay. The thought that keeps running through our mind is "If I could just have [fill in the blank], then I would be happy." The main klesha we experience is craving. The primary suffering in this realm is that we can't accept the alternation of pleasure and pain. Instead, we tend to be obsessed with trying to achieve or maintain comfort.

In the jealous god realm, the balance shifts more heavily toward pleasure than pain. The jealous god has achieved success and good conditions. It seems like there should be nothing to complain about. But the jealous god suffers from a deep-seated insecurity. You keep saying to yourself, "I'm the best," but deep down you feel you're not really the best. So you're always looking around, comparing yourself to others. You want to be in the elite set, among the most beautiful and powerful people. But even if you make it into that set, you're not satisfied. You want to be the elite of the elite. This never stops. You always need to prove you're better than everyone else. With such a mindset, you develop thick armor around your heart, which prevents you from connecting to others.

Like the hungry ghosts, the jealous gods always want more. The major difference is the jealous gods already have so much. But instead of enjoying their good fortune, they dwell in competitiveness, rivalry, one-upmanship, and paranoia. An example in our world might be the leader of a corporation or a powerful country. Some of these people are often in a paranoid state, constantly looking around to see what other company or nation might be gaining power or status. They spend much of their energy trying to make sure no one else gets the upper hand.

Above the jealous gods are the gods, who experience pure, uninterrupted pleasure. They have luxury, comfort, health, wealth, entertainment, and everything else one might want or need. They don't just think "I'm the best," they *know* they're the best. Here the main klesha is pride.

I had some experience of the god realm when I was in high school. I went to a girls' boarding school where the majority of the girls were extremely wealthy. Sometimes I visited their homes during school breaks and met their families. They were so secure in their position and in their thinking that it never crossed their minds that there were other good ways to live. They had not the slightest doubt that their taste was good taste. They also had good politics: they gave to charity and did things to help people and didn't really look down on anyone. But at the same time, they took it for granted that their way was the best way— the only way, really. I loved that school and still have dear friends from that time—intelligent women who have done really good things with their lives. But when I look back I can see the limitations of the god realm mentality.

In the traditional descriptions, the gods live an extremely long life without any suffering. This goes on for so long that it doesn't seem like it could ever end. They take it for granted that they'll remain in this perfect state forever. But as we know, everything comes to an end. At some point, the gods start to show signs of decay. For the first time, it dawns on them that their life as a god is finite. The pain of realizing that they're headed for a lower realm is said to be so great that it rivals the sufferings of the hells.

Trungpa Rinpoche often talked about how you can easily get into a god realm mentality with your spiritual practice. You may aim for—and even achieve—a state of bliss where everything and everyone is beautiful, and all is just as it should be. But this is only a temporary experience, which is cut off from reality. You lose touch with the fact that so many people are suffering. The rawness of life doesn't seem real to you, so other people experiencing that rawness is outside your frame of reference. Thus the practice can turn into a way of becoming oblivious instead of a way of waking up.

Every kind of mentality associated with the realms is a temporary state of mind. We may tend to take up semi-permanent residency in one or two psychological states more frequently than the others, but we are not doomed to be imprisoned by those states of mind. No matter how strong your jealous god tendencies are, for instance, those emotions and mental habits are not as solid and unchanging as they usually feel.

The main thing that keeps us trapped in the experience of any realm—whether hellish or divine or anywhere in between—is our lack of awareness. Therefore, the first step to getting out of a realm is to be conscious that you're in one. For instance, if you're in a hellish frame of mind and think everyone and everything is against you, your unconscious default behavior is to blame. It's the fault of the people who bring you the wrong food, or the ones who open the windows when they should be closed, or the ones who take what belongs to you. It's always the other people, the outer conditions. It's almost as if you have no choice but to be enraged.

Once you become conscious, however, you're already on your way out of the realm. It may not seem like that right away: your awareness will often intensify the emotion at first. But when you start paying attention to what the rage (or the poverty mentality or the ignoring) really feels like, you start finding inner resources. Any of the ways we've discussed about working with kleshas—refraining, transforming, and using them as the path—can serve to get us out of the psychological state we feel trapped in. They can help us see that beyond our emotional turmoil and storylines there is space. At first, we only see this in the pauses and the gaps. But over time, as we continue to practice, our experience of that spaciousness expands. The heart and mind of the practitioner continually expand.

When we become more capable of moving out of our realms, we start to see these styles of imprisonment in a lighter, less solid way. We often identify ourselves with our dominant klesha: "I'm an angry person," "I'm a jealous person," and so on. We do the same thing with others: "He is greedy," "She is arrogant." But nobody is one way and one way only. Our situations are far, far more fluid than that.

Seeing our emotional experiences as temporary states helps us understand that they're not our true identity. Instead, they become evidence that actually we have no fixed true identity. Our true nature is beyond any realm. When we realize this fully, the lid comes off the jar and the bee is liberated.

23

Choosing Our Next Birth

Are the six realms of samsara actual places or are they psychological states? This question immediately brings up an interesting contemplation. Is there really any difference between being in a psychological state and being in an actual place? For instance, is there any meaningful difference between thinking and feeling you're in hell and "actually" being in hell? Is one better than the other, or are they both equally terrible?

Say two people are sitting together in a room. They seem to be seeing and hearing and smelling the same things. However, one is anxious about something that might happen tomorrow, while the other keeps remembering something good that happened this morning. One has a keen sense of smell, while the other has a stuffy nose. One thinks the world is against her, which seems to be confirmed with every experience; the other thinks things are going to get better and better, which seems to be confirmed with every experience. The more we look into this situation, the more we realize these two people sitting in the same room are having radically different experiences.

This gives us an idea how much our "reality" is a projection of our own mind. Though the outer world seems to be one objective reality that everyone can agree on, every individual seems to be living their own private dream. In fact, we might ask ourselves, "In what way is my experience right now different from a dream?" Or even more pointedly, "How do I know I'm not dreaming right now?"

The bardo of becoming is also said to be just like a dream. So in a sense, when we go from the bardo of becoming to our next birth in one of the realms, aren't we simply passing from one dream into another dream? Isn't the whole cycle of life and death and life and death just like an endless dream? These are provocative questions, which I find well worth pondering.

To explore this idea in a more direct way, I like to do the following practice. Choose one thing or a few things that you do regularly in your daily life. It could be brushing your teeth, washing dishes, or driving down a particular road. Or it could be something you regularly see or hear: a certain sign, the door to your apartment, the sound of your phone ringing. Then, whenever you do or see that thing, pause and say, "This is a waking dream." It's a tiny contemplation—just touching in. Let it sink in for a second and then go on with whatever you were doing.

You can say it in different ways: "This is like a dream," or "Is this a dream?" If you keep doing this practice whenever you encounter those prompts, you'll gradually become more accustomed to questioning the solidity of your experience. I've found that when I do this practice a lot, the boundaries between being awake and dreaming start to get fuzzy. Eventually the practice may influence your dreams themselves, so that once in a while you may wake up in the dream and become aware that all you're perceiving isn't real. You know that you're dreaming and that all you perceive is a projection of your own mind. Ideally, this will carry over to the bardo of becoming, when it will be very helpful to have such a perspective in the midst of so much speed and chaos.

The more I do these practices and contemplations, the less certain I am about the distinction between reality and dreams, and between psychological states and actual places. At the same time, whatever words we use, all our experiences do feel totally real, and they matter to us. This is our reality, the realm in which we live.

All beings experience this, but very few—none of the animals, for instance—have access to teachings that can help them wake up from the dream, wake up from their particular style of imprisonment. We humans, on the other hand, have this possibility. Whatever we think will happen in the future and after we die, if we take advantage of these teachings now, we'll be doing ourselves and many others a big favor.

According to the tradition, the bardo of becoming is the intermediate state in which we choose our next rebirth. But here I use the word "choose" lightly. When you're dreaming, do you have much choice where you go and where you turn up? Generally, in our dreams things just happen, and we react according to our habitual patterns. Then again, there are moments when we're not swept along in the story of our dream and when we suddenly realize we do have a choice—to become conscious or to stay asleep.

In the dreamlike bardo of becoming, the pull of karma is also said to be so strong that it generally feels like we have no choices. Most beings are simply swept along toward their next rebirth based on their propensities. The teachings say we become attracted to dim lights that draw us toward rebirth in one of the six realms: whichever one is the most natural continuation of the mentality and tendencies of our former life. But if we have some prior knowledge of the bardo of becoming, we could find ourselves at times recognizing what's going on and being able to make a choice. We might remember that the dim, comforting lights that look so welcoming could lead us to the lower realms, and we might be able to refrain from going any further in that direction.

Trungpa Rinpoche talked about training for the bardos by taking advantage of those times in our life where we're teetering on the "threshold of magic." These are the moments when we have the choice between welcoming the unfamiliar or turning toward the familiar—in other words, the choice between opening up to what's unknown or closing down into habitual behavior.

Right now, because of our comfort orientation, we tend to choose our habitual behavior, even when we're pretty sure it will have a bad result. But we're certainly not destined to make the bad choice every time. Eating the whole box of chocolates or drinking the whole bottle of wine may give you comfort initially, but you realize from experience that after the instant gratification, you'll feel mentally and physically sick. When you keep going with your repetitive behavior, which comes so easily to you, you're guaranteed a painful result. But if you allow the seductive pull of habit to pass through—as difficult as that may be—whatever you do instead will always yield a better result.

In the bardo of becoming, the dim lights start to appear after we've been roaming around for some time, being blown here and there by our karma. At that point, the bardo being, exhausted and desperate for some form of stability, craves a physical body. We've been outside our comfort zone for so long that it's hard to resist anything that seems to represent familiarity and solid ground. Trungpa Rinpoche compared this state of mind to that of a person who's been living on the streets for a long time and feels desperate to get an apartment and settle down.

Unless we make aspirations to be born in a pure realm and we direct our thoughts there during this bardo, we're now due to take another birth in samsara. But it's still not too late to avoid being carried away willy-nilly by the force of our unconscious habits and ending up lost in the lower realms. Again, it's a matter of knowing where to direct our thoughts. The question then becomes, if we can choose a samsaric realm to be born in, which one should we choose?

I, for one, would not choose to be born in the god realm—even though the uninterrupted pleasure that characterizes that realm is what we human beings gener-ally fantasize about. The god realm—whether the actual place or the psychological state—seems to have all of the good things in life and none of the bad. But if our aim is to get out of samsara altogether, such a high level of privilege is not helpful. The all-encompassing pleasure of the gods leaves them out of touch with the difficulties that other people and animals are going through. It's sometimes called the luxury of obliviousness. In such a state, it's hard to feel much compassion or be motivated to change. For this reason, the god realm tends to be a place of spiritual stagnation.

The jealous god realm is less pleasant than the god realm, and certainly no better because the jealous gods are not self-reflective either. And only advanced bodhisattvas would choose to be born in the lower realms, where the suffering is so intense and seamless that there don't seem to be any gaps. Beings in these states are so consumed in their own pain, discomfort, and fear that they have no capacity to look at the deeper causes of their suffering and take steps to find their way out of the whole system. Their entire attention is focused on the painful present moment.

When I think about the pros and cons of each realm in this way, I see that the ideal realm to be born in is the one I'm in right now. This is our precious human life, with all its ups and downs, hopes and disappointments, moments of clarity and moments of confusion. Of course, not every human life is like this. Some people dwell in god-like obliviousness, some dwell in jealous god–like competitiveness, and many more people experience too much suffering to have any mental space for a spiritual path at all. There are countless people who live in places or situations so full of difficulty that there's no luxury of shifting one's attention from the outer world and putting one's effort into inner transformation.

But if you're reading this book, it's likely that you're not in any of these categories. Your life gives you enough pain to spur you on to look for answers and enough comfort to give you some relief. In terms of spiritual growth, the human realm is working well for you: the alternation of happiness and suffering is the perfect balance to provide a fertile ground for awakening. So if you must be reborn in samsara, a life similar to the one you have now is a good one to aim for. In reality, there's an excellent chance your next life will be better than this one. Since all that goes from life to life is your propensities, the positive habits you're cultivating right now will go forward into your next life and benefit the brand new "you."

If our aim is to wake up to our full potential so we can help ourselves and others be free of confusion and fully enjoy our wide-open heart and our brilliant, sky-like mind, then the ideal place to be is right here in the good old human realm.

One major advantage of the human realm is that it gives us a perspective on all the other realms—and on samsara as a whole. Thanks to our diverse experiences of pain and pleasure, as well as our ability to imagine, we have more of a sense of what others are going through. When we're happy, we know what it feels like to be happy, and we can take delight in others' joy and good fortune. And when we experience the inevitable alternation of the human realm and it comes time for us to go through hardship, our discomfort can become a valuable tool for growth.

Our pain can become a window into others' pain and thus help us to develop empathy. Our confusion can open our heart to the confusion of others. Our anxiety can increase our care for others who are anxious. We start to notice how everyone is struggling in one way or another. Maybe it's an animal-like struggle, or maybe it's a jealous god–like struggle, but whatever kind it is, the struggle is difficult and we understand how hard it is to break free. From this perspective, it makes sense to value the human realm and to aspire to be reborn here in our next life. It makes even more sense to aspire to be born into a situation where you'll naturally connect with spiritual teachings and be of most benefit to others. In *The Tibetan Book of the Dead*, there's an aspiration that goes like this: "Wherever I am born, may that land be blessed so that all sentient beings may be happy."

By making aspirations to be born with a precious

human life, we're appreciating the rich, turbulent life we have now. We're acknowledging that, although it's not always easy, our human life gives us exactly what we need for spiritual growth. This appreciation will help us gravitate toward the human realm at the end of the bardo of becoming.

As we prepare for the inevitable end of our lives, there are four main aspirations we can make, which we can think of as plans A through D. Plan A is to attain enlightenment at the moment of death by merging the child luminosity with the mother luminosity (see chapters 5 through 7). Plan B is to awaken in the bardo of dharmata by merging with the brilliant lights or with the deity (see chapter 17). Plan C is to be reborn in a pure realm, where we can make swift progress on the path (see chapter 20). Finally, plan D is to take rebirth as a human being with the conditions most conducive to spiritual progress.

I feel that if we accomplish any of these aspirations, we can say our life has been well spent. On the other hand, the potential for complete awakening is not some distant prospect; it is something achievable in the near future by people like you and me. I once had a conversation about this subject with His Holiness the Seventeenth Karmapa, Ogyen Trinley Dorje, a profound teacher who is very dear to me. I asked him what pure realm I should aspire to be reborn in, and he considered this for a while. Then he said, "Well, Amitabha's pure realm, Sukhavati, is very good. But why not just skip all that and let the mother and child luminosity meet?" I feel that was a tall order, but I've kept it as very precious heart advice.

24

———

Helping Others
with Death and Dying

When my mother passed away, I wasn't able to get there until after she had died, but Trungpa Rinpoche told me it wasn't too late to help her. He suggested I sit by her body and tell her what a good mother she had been and how much I loved her. He recommended sharing fond memories of our being together and saying anything I could to make her feel happy and relaxed.

Trungpa Rinpoche's other key piece of advice was to keep reminding my mother that she had died so she could let go of her life and not feel like she needed to hang around. I was able to follow his advice. I felt touched to be alone with her in the funeral home in this way, and I had the sense that I was easing her mind and helping her make the transition.

What I did with my mother was based on the Tibetan view that the consciousness stays close to the body for a certain period after death. Although the physical body is dead, the consciousness is still very aware of what's happening. This view is also shared by many hospice workers I've spoken to. After someone has died, hospice workers do their best to maintain a peaceful atmosphere. They're careful about what they say and about how they treat the body and the person's belongings.

When people ask me how they can help others through the process of dying and the bardos, I often start by telling them this story. Whatever your beliefs are, the overall idea is to be sensitive that the person is going through a major transition. From the moment they find out they're dying, they will go through many intense experiences, and the best thing we can do is to be open and sensitive and present with whatever arises. Whether they're in a state of advanced dementia or in a coma or have just passed away, we should behave as if they're aware of our presence and try to be with them in a strong, loving, steady way.

Mother Teresa founded her hospice in Kolkata, India, based on the simple idea of making sure people felt loved when they died. She picked up people off the street who would have died without a single person caring about them, and she brought them in to her hospice so they could live their last days in a peaceful, loving environment. If we can keep this simple motivation in mind for the dying and recently deceased people we're connected to, then I think we can do a lot to encourage them and help make their transition a smooth one. Again, we can remember the line from Dzigar Kongtrul Rinpoche's prayer: "May I, with ease and great happiness, let go of all attachments to this life as a son or daughter returning home." This ease and great happiness is what we wish for anyone who is dying or has died. It is also our wish for ourselves.

Within this general advice to be caring and encouraging, many additional things are recommended to help people in the dying process, some of which I will pass on now. From here, I will speak more or less from the Tibetan point of view, but much of this advice can be adapted to align with your own belief system and the person you are caring for.

The first recommendation is to let the dying person know what is happening, stage by stage. If we ourselves are familiar with the signs of outer dissolution, we can let them know, for instance, when the earth element is dissolving. We can tell them that feeling uncomfortably heavy is natural and nothing to fear. This will help them understand that what they're going through is part of the universal dying process.

After the person has physically died, we probably won't be able to tell what stage they're in, but if they're a Buddhist or spiritually inclined, we can read to them from *The Tibetan Book of the Dead*, which is written in the form of a conversation. One traditional way of doing this is to whisper it in the person's ear. You can keep reading the book to them over the forty-nine days of the bardo of becoming. Since a being in this state has some level of clairvoyance, we don't need to be in their physical presence in order to communicate with them. However, if the person is of a different faith—or in life would have had no connection to something as foreign as *The Tibetan Book of the Dead*—then it's best to just talk to them like I did with my mother and help them to feel appreciated. In any case, it's important to remind them often that they have died and can now move on.

A few years ago, I was doing a solitary retreat where my main focus was on the bardo teachings. During that time, a dear friend of mine passed away. Because I was in retreat and had plenty of time, I was able to spend the whole forty-nine days talking to her and reading her *The Tibetan Book of the Dead* and doing whatever I could to encourage her. I wasn't sure what she was going through, but I felt that if I told her these inspiring things about the bardos, she would get it. For the last few years of her life, she'd had Alzheimer's and was confused. But after the elements of this life dissolve, those particular clouds part and the consciousness becomes very receptive to any words of wisdom. This process with my friend informed my whole idea of death. The teachings became much more real for me and inspired me to welcome the challenge of my own transition from this life.

Trungpa Rinpoche taught us that the first three days after someone passes away are especially critical. Since no two people die in exactly the same way, it's hard to be sure just when the final dissolution is taking place. This happens when the element of consciousness dissolves into space. At this moment, we have a chance to attain enlightenment by letting our child luminosity merge with the mother luminosity. In other words, it is a very critical moment. So when any of Rinpoche's students died, we would try to leave their body in place for three days to make sure they had enough time to have both the plan A and plan B opportunities: at the dissolution and during the bardo of dharmata. We would sit in meditation with them and also do tonglen. If it wasn't possible to leave their body in place for so long, we would do our best to adapt to whatever situation arose, emphasizing the need to keep an open and encouraging mind as a favorable atmosphere for the deceased.

At some point while the deceased was thought to be in the bardo of becoming, we would do what's known as a Sukhavati ceremony. This is named after Amitabha's pure land, which is a place where people can aspire to be reborn. In this ceremony, we would burn their photograph as well as a piece of paper with their name on it. The idea is that they would see this happening, and it would help them understand they had died and give them gentle encouragement to move on. We would reassure them that they could let go and that everything and everybody would be just fine. Doing this ceremony increases the likelihood that they will wake up in the dreamlike bardo of becoming and be able to choose a favorable birth, whether in a pure realm or as a human being who will have access to a spiritual path.

Of course, even for someone who has these beliefs and would like such practices and ceremonies performed on their behalf, there's always a chance that things won't turn out as planned. You might die suddenly while you're traveling, or you might be hooked up to a lot of loud machines, or your family members might get into an argument beside your body and ruin the tranquil atmosphere. There are a thousand things that could go wrong. So if you want to have a peaceful death, the best way to ensure that happens is to cultivate a peaceful mind while you're still alive, to practice not getting so upset when unwelcome things enter your life.

Another thing to consider when someone dies is how to relate to their possessions. If we think about how attached we are to some of the things that belong to us, we'll understand how much it could disturb a dead person if we treat their belongings carelessly. It may be unrealistic to keep every little thing they cherished and maintain it in pristine condition, but whatever we do, we should keep in mind their attachments and do our best to treat their possessions with respect and at least not quarrel over them. If we can do this for forty-nine days, that's the best.

I've started working on my own attachments to possessions to lessen the chance that they'll disturb me in the bardo. I have a list of what things should go to what person, but I'm also trying to give them away before I die. When I think of how ruffled I've become when I've lost trivial things like water bottles, I realize that the more I can loosen my grip ahead of time, the better chance I'll have of making it successfully through the bardos.

One of my favorite stories is of a monk who was so dedicated to letting go of his attachments before he died that he'd given away almost all his possessions. At the moment before death, he noticed his teacup sitting on his bedside table and motioned to his friend to hand it to him. Throwing the teacup out the window was his last act on earth.

In whatever way someone dies, there are ways to benefit them, even after much time has passed. We can do virtuous acts and dedicate them to their well-being— wherever they are and whatever form they may have taken. Giving money to people who are destitute, helping animals, visiting a lonely elderly neighbor, just smiling at someone: anything you do on others' behalf, you can also wish for it to help the person who is dying or has passed away.

When my father died, my first Buddhist teacher, Lama Chimé Rinpoche, instructed me to offer my father his favorite food and drink for forty-nine days. Following this advice, I put the offerings by my shrine every morning, and every evening I threw them out in a clean place where they wouldn't be trampled on. I learned later that this is based on the belief that in the bardo of becoming, the dead may experience hunger and thirst but can only get satisfaction from food and drink that are specifically offered to them. I don't know if this is true, but I do know that every morning when I put out the food and drink, I felt a special closeness to my father that I will always cherish. Since then, I've done this practice for many people. When my dear friend died, I offered her a daily feast of espresso and chocolate. For me, it will be hot water and apple pie.

You can also do tonglen. For instance, if the dying or deceased person is a loved one, first take a moment to think of them with great love. Then think about any discomfort, fear, or confusion they might be having—anything that would make them unhappy—and breathe it in with the wish that they could be free of it all. When you breathe out, send them all your love and caring and everything that could make them happy or bring them relief.

I still do these things for my parents even though they're long gone. I don't know for sure that it helps them, but it certainly helps me. And because we've been so closely connected, I feel that it has a positive effect on their minds as well, wherever they may be.

Finally, it's crucial to let yourself fully grieve the loss of anyone close to you. There are no Buddhist teachings that say you shouldn't miss people and that you should just move on as if nothing big has happened. Even though they say that consciousness continues after death and that people with positive propensities will have favorable re-births, grief is a natural and beautiful human emotion. It's uncomfortable when grief swells up and overcomes you, but as time passes, the sadness becomes less and less intense. But every once in a while, out of nowhere, you'll think of the person you lost and you'll cry, which is a good thing. It's a sign of love.

Letting yourself grieve allows you to gradually let go. It allows the flow of impermanence to continue. Of course, we know impermanence never stops, but we have a magical ability to freeze things in our mind and get stuck in the past. Grieving fully allows us to move on with our life when we feel ready to move on.

Trungpa Rinpoche often spoke about the "genuine heart of sadness," which is a tender, open place where you feel connected to people and receptive to the world. This is a positive state of mind that can accompany grief. When I've been in a state of grief, I've experienced this feeling of connection and appreciation with others, even when I don't know them and will never see them again. I remember once when I was grieving going to the post office and feeling overwhelming love for all the other people in line. Unlike many other painful emotions, such as anger and jealousy, sadness and grief tend to connect us more than separate us. Perhaps it's because sadness makes us more tuned in to the universal impermanence of all aspects of our lives: days turning into nights, fresh blooming flowers fading, children growing up, friends and relatives aging, ourselves growing old.

At the same time, we can keep in mind the teaching on the two truths. On the relative level, everything changes and everyone dies. All people and all things are as transitory as clouds, and this can break our hearts. But on the absolute level, nothing dies. Life after life, our bodies come and go, but our true nature always remains the same. It is like space itself: vast and indestructible and full of potential for life to manifest.

25

Waking Up in the Bardo

These teachings are concerned with how to make our life meaningful and transform all that happens to us into the path of awakening. How we respond to the momentary, changeable circumstances of a daily life matters equally now and when we die. As Trungpa Rinpoche said, "The present situation is important. That's the whole point, the important point."

Seeing life as a series of bardos is a very helpful practice. The past has gone, the future hasn't come, and we can't quite catch the in-between moment—yet it is really all there is. I've learned that we can develop our ability to notice the gaps, the pauses, the open space between any two situations. We can start to get the feeling of being in a life that continually begins and ends. This can become a practice of ongoing awareness. The end of *this* is also the beginning of *that*. The idea of rebirth is not purely the idea of physical birth and death. Rebirth takes place every moment, and we could begin to see it like that.

When we meditate, we could notice the space between thoughts. We could notice the gap between one emotion and the next. We could notice the gap between sleeping and waking, the ongoing sense of presence and absence, of coming and going. The gap when we drop a cup, or almost slip, or get bad news, or have a sudden shock.

I wake up in the morning and there's a space between sleeping and not yet being fully awake. I sit up to meditate and it's a fresh experience. Then it's over. I walk into the bathroom, relieve myself, splash cold water on my face, and then that ends. I walk to the kitchen and a new life begins: boiling water, making breakfast, taking my medications. That ends and I'm sitting down and eating.

One lifetime after another, a steady flow of new beginnings and new endings. Trungpa Rinpoche once described his experience of going to the gas station and it sounded like the most fascinating experience one could ever wish for. Driving up and stopping the car. Gap. Turning off the engine. Gap. Rolling down the window and saying, "Fill her up." (That used to happen—really!) Gap. Waiting. Gap. Then finally driving away—going from that bardo to the next, from one wondrous experience to the next.

In life we have a choice of either living in our usual unaware way—lost in our thoughts, run around by our emotions—or waking up and experiencing everything freshly, as if for the very first time. We also have the choice of relating bravely to the underlying groundlessness of our situation rather than trying to avoid it. It is said that this all-pervasive groundlessness has three aspects: uncertainty, vulnerability, and insecurity. How we relate to these feelings now will be how we relate to them in death.

When we are dying, uncertainty, vulnerability, and insecurity can intensify, and we have the choice to desperately hold on or to let go into the freshness that comes with the dissolution. A completely open space becomes available to us if we don't panic but let go—or if we panic, relax with that. This can be a time of full awakening, and it mainly depends on our ease or unease with groundlessness. Even just a moment of relaxation as we die will serve us well.

In the bardo of dharmata, we might experience fear of being drawn into a bigger world, so depending on how we've trained in life, we'll either be drawn into the toned-down, familiar world of suffering, or choose the stretch and let go into a bigger vision. Even if afraid, we can stay with that and let ourselves be afraid. If, in life, we're trained in being okay with what we're feeling, then we'll be okay with what we're feeling in this bardo.

If we arrive in the bardo of becoming, a key instruction is this: try not to run, but hold steady. If we panic, we can stay with the panic and resist the tendency to make any quick moves. In all the bardos of life and death, a key instruction is "Don't struggle." Whatever is happening, stay there—right with what you're feeling. Slow down and pay attention. Develop the capacity to stay in those uncomfortable, edgy places of uncertainty, vulnerability, and insecurity. Develop the capacity to flow with the continual change from bardo to bardo, from gap to gap.

Trungpa Rinpoche used to urge us to "hold our seat." That's what will help us most—that and looking around and realizing there are others with us who are equally panicking, equally trying to run away, equally in need of comfort and love. Emotions can either drag us into realms where we do not want to be or they can link us heart to heart with all our fellow interconnected beings.

Our task is to open to our present situation, along with that of our fellow human beings. Our task, in life and death, is to realize we always have a choice. We can fall asleep into unawareness and stay stuck in the repeating cycle of samsara, or we can wake up. And that, as Dzigar Kongtrul Rinpoche says, is "up to you."

Conclusion

I shi was the last of his tribe. The Yahi had been all but exterminated during and after the Gold Rush. With a few remaining family members, Ishi had fled to the wilderness, and decades later he was the only Yahi left. Early one morning in 1911, he appeared, disoriented and almost naked, in the northern California town of Oroville. Not long after, the anthropologist Alfred Kroeber took the train to Oroville and brought Ishi back to Berkeley, where Kroeber was a professor. He wanted to spend as much time with Ishi as possible, to learn everything he could about him. And by all accounts, Ishi was happy to go along.

Ishi was friendly and warm-hearted, and people were amazed at his adaptability. He was always watching how people did things, figuring out how to live in a completely different world. When someone gave him a coat and tie to wear, he was happy to wear these strange clothes. But when offered shoes, he politely refused. He wanted to feel the earth.

Although some contemporary people feel that Kroeber took advantage of Ishi—and certainly one could interpret it that way—evidence suggests that they became extremely close friends. Eventually, they were able to communicate with words. But when Kroeber asked him his name, he wouldn't say. It was not his custom to tell his name to anyone outside his tribe. So Kroeber called him "Ishi," which simply means "man," and Ishi accepted that.

When Kroeber had first brought him to the station, Ishi hid behind a pillar when the train arrived. Then he came out and they boarded the train together. Later, when they could speak to each other, Kroeber asked him why he had hidden. Ishi said, "We used to see trains from the mountains with their fire and billowing smoke, and we thought they were monsters that ate people. So we always stayed far away from them." Then Kroeber asked, "How did you have the courage to get on the train?" Ishi then said something that I've always found inspiring: "I was more curious than afraid."

One of my main intentions in writing this book has been to help people become "more curious than afraid," especially when it comes to death and dying. To fear death is a daily burden, and, as I've tried to explain, an unnecessary one. Death is part of the ongoing and endless series of bardos, the wondrous flow of birth and death. In order to be fully intimate with life, I feel we have to be fully intimate with death.

Ishi must have been fully intimate with death to behave the way he did. It's not that surprising: All the people he knew had died and he'd been living for years on the edge of starvation. He had nothing left to lose. But if we tune in to how birth and death happen in every moment, we'll realize we also have nothing to lose. Then we'll be able to live fearlessly and with great compassion for all the other people on this planet who are struggling, anxious, and afraid. And our freedom of heart and mind will make us more available to help others and more effective in doing so.

Like many spiritual traditions, Buddhism originated from the universal human need to make a relationship with death. The future Buddha spent his early life within the walls of his father's palace, sheltered from all signs of mortality. But when he ventured out one day, he saw an old man, a sick man, and a corpse. These sights made him wonder what the whole point of life was if it would just lead to these results. He left the comforts of his palace to seek a way of making both life and death more meaningful. What he discovered in his quest and passed down through all the centuries and generations is the wisdom that I've been so fortunate to receive from my teachers. It is this wisdom that, in some small part, I've attempted to convey in this book.

What I've presented about the bardos is only a tiny fraction of the knowledge that you can find in other places. For those who are interested, I've included a suggested reading list at the end of this book. At the same time, I believe the most important factor in preparing for death is to remember that how we live is how we die. If we learn to embrace impermanence, to work with our kleshas, to recognize the sky-like nature of our mind, and to open ourselves wider and wider to the experiences of life, we'll be learning both how to live and how to die. If we develop a passion to learn about the groundless, unpredictable, unfathomable nature of our world and of our mind, that will enable us to face our death with more curiosity than fear.

This precious human birth, so free and well favored, bless me that I reach its full meaning. The time of death is uncertain. Bless me that I have no regrets.

—Prayer to MACHIK LABDRÖN, KARMA CHAGMÉ

A History of the Bardo Teachings

The traditional story of how the bardo teachings came to us is quite extraordinary. In the eighth century, King Trisong Detsen of Tibet wanted to establish Buddhism firmly in his country. A devoted practitioner of the Dharma, he thought he could best serve his subjects by promoting the Buddha's teachings, which were fairly new in Tibet. At that time, Tibet was a wild place. The people themselves were not very tame and there were spirits and demons that created obstacles for the Dharma to take root there. The king wanted to build a magnificent Buddhist temple, but every night the spirits would take apart the construction and put all the earth and stones back where they came from.

Then the king heard about Guru Rinpoche, the powerful enlightened teacher in India, who had the ability to tame the untamable. Guru Rinpoche came to pacify the troublemakers, and Samye Temple, which exists to this day, was built. While in Tibet, Guru Rinpoche performed all kinds of deeds to help plant deep roots of Dharma. He taught many students, helping them to attain high levels of spiritual realization. Some of his teachings, known as *terma* (literally, "treasures"), were intended for future generations, who would encounter them freshly when they were most needed. Yeshe Tsogyal, his consort and closest student, wrote down these teachings, and she and Guru Rinpoche hid them all over Tibet. Guru Rinpoche empowered his twenty-five main disciples to discover these terma in future lifetimes. These disciples, it is said, have been reborn many times over the years as *tertöns*, or treasure discoverers. Chögyam Trungpa Rinpoche was known as a tertön and one of his discoveries was the *Sadhana of Mahamudra*, a practice that many of his students still do regularly.

Bardo Tödrol is part of a terma discovered in the fourteenth century by Karma Lingpa in the Gampo hills of central Tibet. (Gampo Abbey, the monastery in Nova Scotia where I gave some of the teachings adapted for this book, is named after the famous teacher Gampopa, who built his monastery in the Gampo hills.) For a long time after it was discovered, *Bardo Tödrol* was kept secret. Teachers would pass it down to one student at a time. Eventually it was more openly taught, and in the 1920s, an American anthropologist named Walter Evans-Wentz organized its first publication in English with the inaccurate but alluring title *The Tibetan Book of the Dead*. It became wildly popular in the West. In the 1960s, it was taken up enthusiastically by the hippies, of which I was one. It continues to be one of the most widely taught Buddhist texts on the bardos.

Practices

BASIC SITTING MEDITATION

The technique of sitting meditation called *shamatha-vipashyana* ("tranquility-insight") is like a golden key that helps us to know ourselves. In shamatha-vipashyana meditation, we sit upright with legs crossed and eyes open, hands resting on our thighs. Then we simply become aware of our breath as it goes out. It requires precision to be right there with that breath. On the other hand, it's extremely relaxed and extremely soft. Saying "Be right there with the breath as it goes out" is the same thing as saying "Be fully present." Be right here with whatever is going on. Being aware of the breath as it goes out, we may also be aware of other things going on—sounds on the street, the light on the walls. These things may capture our attention slightly, but they don't need to draw us off. We can continue to sit right here, aware of the breath going out.

But being with the breath is only part of the technique. These thoughts that run through our mind continually are the other part. We sit here talking to ourself. The instruction is that when you realize you've been thinking, you label it "thinking." When your mind wanders off, you say to yourself, "Thinking." Whether your thoughts are violent or passionate or full of ignorance and denial; whether your thoughts are worried or fearful; whether your thoughts are spiritual thoughts, pleasing thoughts of how well you're doing, comforting thoughts, uplifting thoughts—whatever they are, without judgment or harshness simply label it all "thinking," and do that with honesty and gentleness.

The touch on the breath is light: Only about 25 percent of the awareness is on the breath. You're not grasping or fixating on it. You're opening, letting the breath mix with the space of the room, letting your breath just go out into space. Then there's something like a pause, a gap until the next breath goes out again. While you're breathing in, there could be some sense of just opening and waiting. It is like pushing the doorbell and waiting for someone to answer. Then you push the doorbell again and wait for someone to answer. Then probably your mind wanders off and you realize you're thinking again—at this point, use the labeling technique.

It's important to be faithful to the technique. If you find that your labeling has a harsh, negative tone to it, as if you were saying, "Dammit!"—that you're giving yourself a hard time—say it again and lighten up. It's not like trying to shoot down the thoughts as if they were clay pigeons. Instead, be gentle. Use the labeling part of the technique as an opportunity to develop softness and compassion for yourself. Anything that comes up is okay in the arena of meditation. The point is, you can see it honestly and make friends with it.

Although it is embarrassing and painful, it is very healing to stop hiding from yourself. It is healing to know all the ways that you're sneaky; all the ways that you hide out, criticize people; all the ways that you shut down, deny, close off; all your weird little ways. You can know all that with some sense of humor and kindness. By knowing yourself, you're coming to know humanness altogether. We are all up against these things. We are all in this together. When you realize that you're talking to yourself, label it "thinking" and notice your tone of voice. Let it be compassionate and gentle and humorous. Then you'll be changing old stuck patterns that are shared by the whole human race. Compassion for others begins with kindness to ourselves.

The length of time you sit is up to you. It can be as short as ten minutes or as long as you like. This is a practice for the bardo of this life and for the bardo of dying, and it will come in handy for all the other bardos as well.

MEDITATING WITH OPEN AWARENESS: A GUIDED PRACTICE BY YONGEY MINGYUR RINPOCHE

Nonmeditation is the best meditation. In real meditation, you do not have to meditate. Just let your mind rest as it is. Whatever the state of your mind is, peaceful, not peaceful, thoughts or no thoughts, it does not matter. The background of all this is awareness, right? So just be with awareness, allowing it. Whatever thoughts or emotions arise, accept or allow them and just be. As long as you do not become unconscious or completely lost, it is okay.

So, we will do this practice. This is also what we call "open presence meditation." Sometimes we call it "meditation without an object." There are a few different names. Some traditional texts call it "meditation without support."

Please sit in your meditation posture. First, we will practice with a gentle out-breath. Breathe in and breathe out naturally. At the end of the out-breath, there is a natural pause. Simply rest in open awareness during this pause. When you feel the need to, inhale once again. Relax as you breathe in and breathe out. Breathe naturally, simply resting in awareness during the pause at the end of each out-breath. See if you notice these pauses naturally becoming a little longer. Keep your meditation posture. Do not force anything. Breathe in, breathe out, and rest in the pause.

Okay, how was that? Now, we will try it without pausing the breath, just completely natural. You do not have to do anything with the breath. Let the mind just rest. Just be with a sense of presence.

When you rest like that, you are not lost. There is awareness, but the awareness does not have a particular object. You are just relaxing. Some people might find some sense of presence, of being. Something is there. You cannot really describe it, but you are not lost. You are not meditating, but also not lost. Okay? That is all.

TONGLEN

Tonglen practice, also known as "taking and sending," reverses our usual logic of avoiding suffering and seeking pleasure. In tonglen practice, we visualize taking in the pain of others with every in-breath and sending out whatever will benefit them on the out-breath. In the process, we become liberated from age-old patterns of selfishness. We begin to feel love for both ourselves and others; we begin to take care of ourselves and others.

Tonglen awakens our compassion and introduces us to a far bigger view of reality. It introduces us to the unlimited spaciousness of *shunyata* (emptiness). By doing the practice, we begin to connect with the open dimension of our being.

Tonglen can be done for those who are ill, those who are dying or have died, or those who are in pain of any kind. It can be done as a formal meditation practice or right on the spot at any time. If we are out walking and we see someone in pain, we can breathe in that person's pain and send out relief to them.

Usually, we look away when we see someone suffering. Their pain brings up our fear or anger; it brings up our resistance and confusion. So we can also do tonglen for all the people just like ourselves—all those who wish to be compassionate but instead are afraid, who wish to be brave but instead are cowardly. Rather than beating ourselves up, we can use our personal stuckness as a stepping stone to understanding what people are up against all over the world. Breathe in for all of us and breathe out for all of us. Use what seems like poison as medicine. We can use our personal suffering as the path to compassion for all beings.

When you do tonglen as a formal meditation practice, it has four stages.

1. Flash on Bodhichitta
Rest your mind for a second or two in a state of openness or stillness. This stage is traditionally called "flashing on absolute bodhichitta," "awakened heart-mind," or "opening to basic spaciousness and clarity."

2. Begin the Visualization
Work with texture. Breathe in feelings of heat, darkness,

and heaviness—a sense of claustrophobia—and breathe out feelings of coolness, brightness, and light—a sense of freshness. Breathe in completely, taking in negative energy through all the pores of your body. When you breathe out, radiate positive energy completely, through all the pores of your body. Do this until your visualization is synchronized with your in- and out-breaths.

3. Focus on a Personal Situation

Focus on any painful situation that's real to you. Traditionally you begin by doing tonglen for someone you care about and wish to help. However, if you are stuck, you can do the practice for the pain you are feeling yourself, and simultaneously for all those who feel the same kind of suffering. For instance, if you are feeling inadequate, breathe that in for yourself and all the others in the same boat and send out confidence, adequacy, and relief in any form you wish.

4. Expand Your Compassion

Finally, make the taking in and sending out bigger. If you are doing tonglen for someone you love, extend it out to all those who are in the same situation. If you are doing tonglen for someone you see on television or on the street, do it for all the others in the same boat. Make it bigger than just that one person. You can do tonglen for people you consider to be your enemies—those who hurt you or hurt others. Do tonglen for them, thinking of them as having the same confusion and stuckness as your friend or yourself. Breathe in their pain and send them relief.

Tonglen can extend infinitely. As you do the practice, your compassion naturally expands over time, and so does your realization that things are not as solid as you thought, which is a glimpse of emptiness. As you do this practice, gradually at your own pace, you will be surprised to find yourself more and more able to be there for others, even in what used to seem like impossible situations.

Charts

STAGES OF DISSOLUTION

Stage 1	Earth into Water Feel heavy, weighted down Sight goes Secret sign: shimmering mirage
Stage 2	Water into Fire Feel thirsty; can't control body fluids Hearing goes Secret sign: smoke
Stage 3	Fire into Air Feel cold; can't get warm Smell goes Secret sign: fireflies, sparks of light

Stage 4	Air into Consciousnes
	Hard to breathe; short inhalation, long exhalation
	Taste goes
	Secret sign: butter-lamp or torch-like image
Stage 5	Consciousness into Space
	Outer respiration ceases
	Touch goes
	Secret sign: butter-lamp image continues
Then	Inner Dissolution
	The body is dead
	Inner respiration ceases at third stage (below)
	Consciousness dies in three stages (subtle, more subtle, most subtle)
	1. Appearance: White. Like pure sky filled with moonlight. Anger dissolves.
	2. Increase: Red. Everything appears red. Passion and craving dissolve.
	3. Attainment: Black. We either "black out" or recognize the true nature of mind (mother and child luminosity meet).
	At the end of the inner dissolution, consciousness leaves the body.

THE FIVE BUDDHA FAMILIES

Symbol	VAJRA	RATNA
Element	Water	Earth
Color*	White	Yellow
Direction	East	South
Season	Winter	Autumn
Wisdom Aspect	Mirror-Like Wisdom sharp, precise, clear, seeing, *prajna* (discriminating awareness), indestructibility, intellectual	Wisdom of Equanimity richness, plentiful, generous, extends themselves, magnetizing, making yourself at home
Neurosis Aspect†	Aggression intellectual fixation, cold, critical, cutting	Pride ostentatious, expands needlessly, never enough, overdoes it

* Note that there are differing traditions surrounding the colors and other attributes associated with each of the buddha families.

† The neurosis aspect can be transmuted into its wisdom (or enlightened) aspect.

PADMA	KARMA	BUDDHA
Fire	Air	Space
Red	Green	Blue
West	North	Center of the mandala
Summer	Spring	———
Discriminating Wisdom compassionate, hospitality, openness, inquisitiveness, accommodating	All-Accomplishing Wisdom actions fulfill their purpose easily	Dharmadhatu Wisdom spacious, steady, wise, contemplative, foundation of basic space
Craving seduces and charms for ego's sake, false smile, wants everyone to like them	Jealousy highly irritable, critical, overefficient, speedy, wants to create a uniform, neat world	Ignorance spacey, lazy, couldn't care less, depressed, do what takes the least effort, dull

The six realms of samsara depicted above are, clockwise from the top: the god realm, the jealous god realm, the hungry ghost realm, the hell realm, the animal realm, and the human realm. The bird, snake, and pig at the center of the circle represent the three main kleshas of craving, aggression, and ignorance. These emotions give rise to the states of mind and actions that create our experience in samsara. In the middle ring, between the six realms (on the outside) and the representation of the three main kleshas (in the center), the left half of the ring represents positive actions that lead to birth in the higher realms and the right half of the ring represents negative actions that lead to birth in the lower realms.

Suggestions for Further Reading

Anam Thubten. *A Sacred Compass*. Point Richmond, CA: Dharmata Foundation, 2020.

Anyen Rinpoche. *Dying with Confidence: A Tibetan Buddhist Guide to Preparing for Death*. Boston: Wisdom Publications, 2014.

Chögyam Trungpa. *Journey without Goal: The Tantric Wisdom of the Buddha*. Boston: Shambhala Publications, 2010. First edition 1981.

Chögyam Trungpa. *Transcending Madness: The Experience of the Six Bardos*. Boston: Shambhala Publications, 1999. First edition 1992.

Chögyam Trungpa and Francesca Fremantle. *The Tibetan Book of the Dead: The Great Liberation through Hearing in the Bardo*. Boulder: Shambhala Publications, 2019. First edition 1975.

Dzogchen Ponlop. *Emotional Rescue*. New York: Tarcher-Perigee, 2016.

Dzogchen Ponlop. *Mind Beyond Death*. Ithaca, NY: Snow Lion Publications, 2008.

Dzongsar Jamyang Khyentse. *Living Is Dying: How to Pre-*

pare for Death, Dying, and Beyond. Boulder: Shambhala Publications, 2020.

Fremantle, Francesca. *Luminous Emptiness*. Boston: Shambhala, 2003.

Holecek, Andrew. *Preparing to Die*. Boston: Snow Lion, 2013.

McLeod, Ken. *Reflections on Silver River: Tokmé Zongpo's Thirty-Seven Practices of a Bodhisattva*. Los Angeles: Unfettered Mind Media, 2013.

McLeod, Ken. *Wake Up to Your Life: Discovering the Buddhist Path of Attention*. San Francisco: Harper San Francisco, 2002.

Saunders, George. *Lincoln in the Bardo: A Novel*. New York: Random House, 2018.

Sogyal Rinpoche. *The Tibetan Book of Living and Dying*. San Francisco: Harper San Francisco, 1992.

Tulku Thondup. *Peaceful Death, Joyful Rebirth*. Boston: Shambhala Publications, 2007.

Yongey Mingyur and Helen Tworkov. *In Love with the World: A Monk's Journey through the Bardos of Living and Dying*. New York: Random House, 2019.

Acknowledgments

I want to begin by acknowledging my beloved teachers, without whom I'd have no clue what any of these bardo teachings mean. Next, I'd like to thank Yongey Mingyur Rinpoche for his powerful example and for giving me permission to use his meditation on open awareness. Erik Pema Kunsang and Francesca Fremantle clarified some of the more difficult aspects of the bardo teachings. Helen Tworkov answered questions about Mingyur Rinpoche's story. Sarah Stanton of Shambhala Publications made many valuable suggestions to help this book connect to its audience; Nikko Odiseos and Ivan Bercholz of Shambhala provided valuable leadership and support. Barbara Abrams, one of my most faithful readers, read an early draft of the manuscript and provided insightful feedback. Finally, I'd like to give a special thanks to my friend and dharma brother Joseph Waxman for taking the transcripts of my talks and doing the heroic job of turning them into this book. It is always a great pleasure to work with my heart friend Joey Waxman.

Index

relationship between, 53–55
See also absolute truth; relative truth

Vairochana, 96, 104
Vajra family, 95–96, 98, 99, 100, 190
Vajrayana, 109–10
virtual reality test, 16–17
vulnerability, 14, 17, 172, 173

warmth, two kinds, 139, 142
Western medicine, 25
When Things Fall Apart, 127
wisdom, 37
    co-emergent, 48, 88, 89, 91–92, 94–95
    display of, 111
    five main types, 92–93, 190–91
    in kleshas' energy, 71, 74, 87, 88, 89–90, 105–6, 190–91
    See also all-accomplishing wisdom; dharmadhatu wisdom; discriminating wisdom; mirror-like wisdom; wisdom of equanimity
wisdom of equanimity, 93–94, 96, 100, 104, 191

Yeshe Tsogyal, 180

About the Author

ANI PEMA CHÖDRÖN was born Deirdre Blomfield-Brown in 1936, in New York City. She attended Miss Porter's School in Connecticut and graduated from the University of California at Berkeley. She taught as an elementary school teacher for many years in both New Mexico and California. Ani Pema has two children and three grandchildren.

While in her mid-thirties, Ani Pema traveled to the French Alps and encountered Lama Chimé Rinpoche, with whom she studied for several years. She became a novice nun in 1974 while studying with Lama Chimé in London. His Holiness the Sixteenth Karmapa came to Scotland at that time, and Ani Pema received her ordination from him.

Ani Pema first met her root guru, Chögyam Trungpa Rinpoche, in 1972. Lama Chimé encouraged her to work with Rinpoche, and it was with him that she ultimately made her most profound connection, studying with him from 1974 until his death in 1987. At the request of the Sixteenth Karmapa, she received the full bhikshuni ordination in the Chinese lineage of Buddhism in 1981 in Hong

Kong. She served as the director of Karma Dzong in Boulder, Colorado, until moving in 1984 to rural Cape Breton, Nova Scotia, to be the director of Gampo Abbey. Chögyam Trungpa Rinpoche gave her explicit instructions on establishing this monastery for Western monks and nuns.

Ani Pema currently teaches in the United States and Canada and plans for an increased amount of time in solitary retreat under the guidance of Venerable Dzigar Kongtrul Rinpoche. She is interested in helping to establish Tibetan Buddhist monasticism in the West, as well as continuing her work with Western Buddhists of all traditions, sharing ideas and teachings. Her nonprofit, the Pema Chödrön Foundation, was set up to assist in this purpose, as well as to support Tibetan Buddhist nuns in India and Nepal and organizations that help at-risk individuals and populations in the United States.

She has written several books, including *Welcoming the Unwelcome, The Wisdom of No Escape, Start Where You Are, When Things Fall Apart, The Places That Scare You, Becoming Bodhisattvas, Practicing Peace,* and *Living Beautifully.*

Books and Selected Audio
by Pema Chödrön

BOOKS

Awakening Loving-Kindness
We often look far and wide for guidance to become better people, as though the answers were *somewhere out there*. But Pema Chödrön suggests that the best and most direct teacher for awakening loving-kindness is in fact *your very own life*. Based on talks given during a one-month meditation retreat at Gampo Abbey, where Pema lives and teaches, her teachings here focus on learning how to see the events of our lives as the perfect material for learning to love ourselves and our world playfully and wholeheartedly—and to live in our skin fearlessly, without aggression, harshness, or shame.

Becoming Bodhisattvas:
A Guidebook for Compassionate Action
The Way of the Bodhisattva has long been treasured as an indispensable guide to enlightened living, offering a window into the greatest potential within us all. Written in the eighth century by the scholar and saint Shantideva, it

presents a comprehensive view of the Mahayana Buddhist tradition's highest ideal—to commit oneself to the life of a bodhisattva warrior, a person who is wholeheartedly dedicated to the freedom and common good of all beings. In this comprehensive commentary, Pema Chödrön invites you to journey more deeply into this liberating way of life, presenting Shantideva's text verse by verse and offering both illuminating stories and practical exercises to enrich the text and bring its timeless teachings to life in our world today.

Comfortable with Uncertainty:
108 Teachings on Cultivating Fearlessness and Compassion
Collecting some of the most powerful passages from Pema Chödrön's many beloved books, this compact handbook for spiritual practice is rich with inspiration and insight. Here she explores life-changing concepts, themes, and practices from the Buddhist tradition, showing how anyone (not just Buddhists) can draw from them to become more courageous, aware, and kindhearted. It includes the benefits of meditation and mindfulness, letting go of the fixations that weigh us down, working directly with fear and other painful emotions, and much more.

The Compassion Book
Pema Chödrön introduces a powerful, transformative practice called *lojong*, which has been a primary focus of her teachings and personal practice for many years. This book presents fifty-nine pithy slogans from the *lojong* teachings for daily contemplation and includes Pema's clear, succinct guidance on how to understand them—

and how they can enrich our lives. It also features a forty-five minute downloadable audio program titled "Opening the Heart."

Living Beautifully with Uncertainty and Change
We live in difficult times. Life sometimes seems like a roiling and turbulent river threatening to drown us and destroy the world. Why, then, shouldn't we cling to the certainty of the shore—to our familiar patterns and habits? Because, Pema Chödrön teaches, that kind of fear-based clinging keeps us from the infinitely more satisfying experience of being fully alive. The teachings she presents here—known as the "Three Commitments"—provide a wealth of wisdom for learning to step right into the river: to be completely, fearlessly present even in the hardest times, the most difficult situations.

The Places That Scare You:
A Guide to Fearlessness in Difficult Times
We always have a choice in how we react to the circumstances of our lives. We can let them harden us and make us increasingly resentful and afraid, or we can let them soften us and allow our inherent human kindness to shine through. Here Pema Chödrön provides essential tools for dealing with the many difficulties that life throws our way, teaching us how to awaken our basic human goodness and connect deeply with others—to accept ourselves and everything around us complete with faults and imperfections. If we go to the places that scare us, Pema suggests, we just might find the boundless life we've always dreamed of.

The Pocket Pema Chödrön

This treasury of 108 short selections from the best-selling books of Pema Chödrön offers teachings on breaking free of destructive patterns; developing patience, kindness, and joy amid our everyday struggles; becoming fearless; and unlocking our natural warmth, intelligence, and goodness. Designed for on-the-go inspiration, this is a perfect guide to Buddhist principles and the foundations of meditation and mindfulness.

Practicing Peace

In this pocket-size guide to the practice of inner peace, Pema Chödrön shows us how to look deeply at the underlying causes of our tensions and how we really *can* create a more peaceful world—by starting right where we are and learning to see the seeds of hostility in our hearts. She draws on Buddhist teachings to explore the origins of anger, aggression, hatred, and war, and offers practical techniques all of us can use to work for genuine, lasting peace in our own lives and in whatever circumstances we find ourselves.

Start Where You Are:
A Guide to Compassionate Living

Pema here offers down-to-earth guidance on how we can go beyond the fleeting attempts to "fix" our pain and, instead, take our lives as they are as the only path to achieve what we all yearn for most deeply—to embrace rather than deny the difficulties of our lives. These teachings, framed around the fifty-nine traditional Tibetan Buddhist maxims known as the *lojong* slogans—such as "Always meditate on whatever provokes resentment," "Be grateful to everyone," and "Don't expect applause"—point us directly to our own heart and mind. By working with these slogans as everyday meditations, *Start Where You Are* shows how we can all develop the courage to work with our own inner pain and discover true joy, holistic well-being, and unshakable confidence.

Taking the Leap:
Freeing Ourselves from Old Habits and Fears
These classic Buddhist teachings about *shenpa* (painful attachments and compulsions) help us see how certain habits of mind tend to "hook" us and get us stuck in states of anger, blame, self-hatred, and addiction—and how we can liberate ourselves from them. Pema offers insights and practices we can immediately put to use in our lives to take a bold leap toward a new way of living—one that will bring about positive transformation for ourselves and for our troubled world.

Welcoming the Unwelcome:
Wholehearted Living in a Brokenhearted World
In an increasingly polarized world, Pema shows us how to strengthen our abilities to find common ground, even when we disagree, and influence our environment in positive ways. Sharing never before told personal stories from her remarkable life, simple and powerful everyday practices, and directly relatable advice, Pema encourages us all to become triumphant bodhisattvas—compassionate beings—in times of hardship. This book includes teachings

on the true meaning of karma, recognizing the basic goodness in ourselves and the people we share our lives with, and step-by-step guides to a basic sitting meditation and a compassion meditation that anyone can use to bring light to the darkness we face, wherever and whatever it may be.

When Things Fall Apart:
Heart Advice for Difficult Times
How can we live our lives when everything seems to fall apart—when we are continually overcome by fear, anxiety, and pain? The answer, Pema Chödrön suggests, might be just the opposite of what you expect. Here, in her most beloved and acclaimed work, Pema shows that moving *toward* painful situations and becoming intimate with them can open up our hearts in ways we never before imagined. Drawing from traditional Buddhist wisdom, she offers life-changing tools for transforming suffering and negative patterns into habitual ease and boundless joy.

The Wisdom of No Escape:
And the Path of Loving-Kindness
In this guide to true kindness for self and others, Pema Chödrön presents a uniquely practical approach to opening ourselves up to life in all circumstances. She reveals that when we embrace the happiness and heartache, inspiration and confusion, and all the twists and turns that are a natural part of life, we can begin to discover a true wellspring of courageous love that's been within our hearts all along.

AUDIO

Be Grateful to Everyone:
An In-Depth Guide to the Practice of Lojong
One of the best ways to bring meditation off the cushion and into everyday life is to practice *lojong* (or mind training). For centuries, Tibetans have used fifty-nine powerful mind-training slogans as a way to transform life's ordinary situations into opportunities for awakening. Pema Chödrön here presents her definitive audio teachings on *lojong*. She offers an overview of the practice and goes on to provide inspiring commentary on the slogans while paying special attention to how to apply them on the spot in our daily lives.

Don't Bite the Hook:
Finding Freedom from Anger, Resentment,
and Other Destructive Emotions
In this recorded weekend retreat, Pema draws on Buddhist teachings to show us how to relate constructively to the inevitable shocks, losses, and frustrations of life so that we can find true happiness. The key, Pema explains, is not biting the "hook" of our habitual responses.

The Fearless Heart:
The Practice of Living with Courage and Compassion
Pema shows us how to transform negative emotions like fear and guilt into courageous self-acceptance in *The Fearless Heart*. Her teachings are based on five aphorisms presented to Machik Labdrön, one of Tibetan Buddhism's greatest female teachers. Pema offers insightful guidance

on how to remain courageous in the face of pain, and how to increase feelings of generosity and passion through fearlessness. This audio program includes an extensive question-and-answer session and guided meditation practices available for the first time.

Fully Alive: A Retreat with Pema Chödrön on Living Beautifully with Uncertainty and Change
In this recorded weekend retreat, Pema Chödrön and her teaching assistant, Meg Wheatley, teach us to stop clinging to the certainty of life's shore and to instead step right into the river: to be completely, fearlessly present, even in the hardest times, the most difficult situations. That's the secret of being fully alive.

Giving Our Best:
A Retreat with Pema Chödrön on Practicing
the Way of the Bodhisattva
Pema Chödrön teaches on how to nurture a compassionate attitude, using a text that is very close to her heart: the Buddhist classic known as *The Way of the Bodhisattva*. She focuses on its primary subject, the enlightened heart and mind (*bodhichitta*), showing us how this awakened state, which often seems infinitely far out of our grasp, is always available to us right where we are.

Perfect Just as You Are:
Buddhist Practices on the Four Limitless Ones—
Loving-Kindness, Compassion, Joy, and Equanimity
This in-depth study course offers Pema Chödrön's definitive teachings on the Buddhist practice called the "Four

Limitless Ones"—a practice that helps us recognize and grow the seeds of love, compassion, joy, and equanimity already present in our hearts. She offers guided meditations, on-the-spot practices to use in the midst of daily life, an overview of bodhichitta and the bodhisattva vow, guided shamatha meditation, writing and reflection exercises, methods to weaken the grip of negative emotions, and question-and-answer sessions.

Smile at Fear:
A Retreat with Pema Chödrön on Discovering
Your Radiant Self-Confidence
Behind each of our fears resides a basic fear of *ourselves*. In this recorded retreat, Pema Chödrön shares teachings inspired by the book *Smile at Fear*, which was written by her teacher Chögyam Trungpa. Here is a vision for moving beyond this most basic fear of self to discover the innate bravery, trust, and joy that reside at the core of our being.

This Moment Is the Perfect Teacher:
Ten Buddhist Teachings on Cultivating
Inner Strength and Compassion
Lojong is a powerful Tibetan Buddhist practice created especially for training the mind to work with the challenges of everyday living. It teaches our hearts to soften, reframes our attitude toward difficulty, and allows us to discover a wellspring of inner strength. In this recorded retreat, Pema Chödrön introduces the *lojong* teachings and explains how we can apply them to any situation in our life—because, as Pema says, "every moment is an opportunity for awakening."

LIBRARY OF CONGRESS CATALOGING-IN-PUBLICATION DATA

Names: Chödrön, Pema, author. | Waxman, Joseph, editor.
Title: How we live is how we die / Pema Chödrön;
edited by Joseph Waxman.
Description: First edition. | Boulder, Colorado: Shambhala
Publications, Inc., [022] | Includes index.
Identifiers: LCCN 2022003735 | ISBN 9781611809244 (hardback)
Subjects: LCSH: Death—Religious aspects—Buddhism. |
Future life—Buddhism. | Buddhism—Doctrines.
Classification: LCC BQ4487 .C485 2022 |
DDC294.3/423—dc23/eng/20220127
LC record available at https://lccn.loc.gov/2022003735